THE COUNTRY BOY KILLER

THE COUNTRY BOY KILLER

J.T. HUNTER

Pedialaw Press

Copyright

THE COUNTRY BOY KILLER: The True Story of Cody Legebokoff -
Canada's Teenage Serial Killer
Written by J.T. Hunter

Published in United States of America

This is a work of nonfiction. The names of a few witnesses were changed at
their request.

Cover design, formatting and layout by Evening Sky Publishing Services

Print ISBN-13: 978-0-578-71100-3

eBook ISBN-13: 978-0-578-71101-0

Contents

Prologue

He was the friendly, baby-faced, Canadian boy next door. He came from a loving, caring, and well-respected family. Blessed with good looks and backwoods country charm, he was popular with his peers, and although an accident at birth left permanent nerve damage in one of his arms, he excelled in sports. A self-proclaimed "die hard" Calgary Flames fan, he played competitive junior hockey and competed on his school's snowboarding team. And he enjoyed the typical simple pleasures of a boy growing up in the country: camping, hunting, and fishing with family and friends.

But he also enjoyed brutally murdering women, and he would become one of the youngest serial killers in Canadian history.

ONE

A Chance Encounter

During the cold, dark hours of November 27, 2010, Royal Canadian Mounted Police Constable Aaron Kehler drove along a remote stretch of Highway 27 in north-central British Columbia. As Kehler made his way south from Fort St. James toward Vanderhoof, a light snow fell from the moonless, overcast sky. Just after 9:35 p.m., Kehler came to the top of a small ridge on the salted and sanded road when something caught his eye. Out of the darkness, headlights appeared in the distance ahead of him, just to the west of the highway, bobbing up and down as if from a vehicle moving over bumpy terrain at a high rate of speed.

Kehler's first thought was that the vehicle might be a snowmobile since so much snow had fallen in the area recently. However, as he continued heading south toward the headlights, he began to make out a black pickup truck as it sped eastward on a snow-covered, abandoned logging road. Showing no sign of slowing down, the truck emerged from the tree line and darted onto the highway in front of him. The vehicle's high rate of speed caused it to slide into the north-bound lane before the driver regained control, steering it back into the opposite lane and then hastily continuing south.

Red flags immediately went up in Kehler's mind. Feeling that something was not right, he decided to follow the truck until he could meet up with RCMP Constable Kanwalprit Sidhu, who was driving north to meet him. Due to the time of night and remoteness of the area, an area where people tended to be armed, Kehler did not want to confront the driver of the black truck without backup. He matched speeds with the fleeing truck to keep pace with it. Although the posted speed limit was 100 kilometers per hour, his speedometer reflected a speed ranging from 110 to 115.

About nine minutes and ten kilometers later, he spotted Sidhu's vehicle approaching from the south. Kehler quickly activated his emergency lights. After continuing on for a couple hundred meters, the truck gradually slowed down and then pulled over. It was approximately 9:45 p.m.

Kehler, a general duty constable with just over a year of law enforcement experience, had begun his shift a few hours earlier at the RCMP detachment in Fort St. James, a small logging and mining town located on the southeastern shore of Stuart Lake at the end of Highway 27. He had been on his way to meet with Constable Sidhu of the RCMP's Vanderhoof Detachment to retrieve a handbag that had been dropped off there. The bag belonged to one of the passengers in an automobile accident that occurred when a car struck a moose and crashed into a snowbank north of Fort St. James near Pinchi Lake. Kehler and Sidhu had arranged to meet half-way between Vanderhoof and Fort St. James so that Kehler could return the handbag to its owner.

Now Kehler approached the black truck that had appeared seemingly out of nowhere. It was a GMC Sierra pickup with 4x4 decals on the sides and a steel tool box secured against the cabin in the back. Pausing at the rear of the truck, Kehler brushed snow off of the license plate so that he could call it in to dispatch. Then he crept cautiously toward the driver's side door. As he approached the door, he was surprised to see that the driver already had his license and registration in hand and was dangling them out of the window. It struck Kehler as extremely odd. In the over 100 roadside stops that he had made as a police officer, this was the first time that a driver had his license and registration sticking out of the window immediately after being pulled over. Usually the individuals he pulled over were too nervous to have the presence of mind to get the necessary documentation in order. There was just something about sirens and flashing lights that put people on edge.

He stepped up to the driver's window and peered warily inside. A young man who looked like he could still be in high school was the truck's only occupant. Kehler greeted him.

"Good evening, sir. Where are you going in such a hurry?" Kehler asked.

"I'm just on my way to my grandfather's house," the shaggy-haired driver replied cordially.

As the young man offered his explanation, Kehler noticed that he was wearing only black and white plaid shorts and a black, long-sleeve sweater. This also struck Kehler as strange considering the frigid temperature outside. Then he saw a small, red smear on the left side of the driver's chin. It looked like he might have cut himself shaving. Kehler also noticed what seemed to be tiny drops of blood on one of the man's thighs. Glancing further into the truck's cabin, he spotted an open can of Lucky beer tucked in behind the driver's seat.

"I see an open container of alcohol in this vehicle," he informed the driver. "I'm going to need you to step out of the truck so that I can search it."

"Uh, sure," said the young man behind the wheel.

He opened the driver's side door and stepped out. With the driver and truck's cabin in better view, Kehler could see more droplets of blood on the man's legs, and he noticed that the rubber floor mat of the truck was wet. A small puddle of blood had formed where the driver's feet had been. As Kehler glanced at the floor mat, Constable Sidhu's face appeared at the passenger side window.

Like Kehler, Sidhu was a general duty constable, but unlike his younger counterpart, Sidhu had four years of experience with the RCMP. When he had approached the southbound black truck from the northbound lane, Sidhu's radar had clocked the truck's speed at 115 kilometers per hour. After passing by the truck, he had activated his vehicle's emergency lights, made a U-turn, and pulled up behind Kehler, who had already initiated the traffic stop by the time Sidhu caught up to him.

Now Sidhu peered into the passenger side window of the truck, while Kehler spoke to the lightly-clothed driver standing outside at the rear of the vehicle. Kehler figured that the young man wearing shorts must be cold since the outside temperature was between -5 and -10 degrees Celsius. However, he was not simply concerned about the man's comfort. He also wanted the man secured in the back of his police vehicle to ensure Sidhu's and his own safety as they searched the man's truck.

"You'd probably be more comfortable in my truck," Kehler suggested. "It's much warmer in there."

"Yeah, that sounds good," the man replied.

"Alright, I'll have to search you real quick before you get in the truck," Kehler explained. "It's normal procedure."

He patted the young man's shorts and sweater and found a cell phone in one of his pockets. Kehler looked it over and then handed it back to him. As the man climbed into the back seat of the RCMP truck, Kehler noticed a crew-style pocket on the left side of his shorts that he had overlooked. He did a quick pat down of the pocket and found a metal Leatherman multi-tool with several knife blades attached. When Kehler opened the Leatherman tool, he saw an unmistakable red stain on its interior surfaces.

"What's this about?" he asked.

"Oh, I used that on some grouse earlier," the man replied nonchalantly.

"This is way too much blood for a grouse," Kehler countered.

"I had to use it on a deer before that," the man said without batting an eye.

"You killed a deer with it?" Kehler asked incredulously.

"Not exactly."

Kehler paused to allow the man time to provide a further explanation, but none was offered.

"Do you have a hunting license?" Kehler asked.

"No," the young man replied.

Kehler had a hunch that the man was hiding something. He put the Leatherman tool on the hood of his truck and climbed into the back seat, securing the door behind him.

"Because you can't get out – because it's a locked, confined area, it's considered a detention – an investigative detention," Kehler informed the young man. "So tell me in detail why you're out here at this time of night and why all of the blood on the tool."

The detained man told him that he had met a friend of his, Thomas Russell, at around 4:00 p.m. earlier that evening in Vanderhoof. The two drove to a gravel logging road just outside of town and eventually came across a deer. Russell shot the deer in the shoulder with his .306 caliber rifle, but the deer ran off. They eventually tracked it down and killed it.

"Did you use the Leatherman to gut the deer or something?" Kehler asked.

"No, we didn't gut it," the man replied.

The man's story seemed plausible on its face, but Kehler still felt that something about it did not add up.

"So were you poaching then?" he asked.

"Yeah," the man admitted sheepishly.

At the least, Kehler figured that the traffic stop would

result in poaching charges against the young suspect. He decided that it was time to call in a conservation officer from the British Columbia Conservation Service. He noticed Constable Sidhu walking by the vehicle, and waved him over.

"We might be dealing with some poaching here, can we get conservation called out?"

Sidhu nodded and continued on to his truck to make the call. Just then, the poaching suspect spoke up.

"I need to get back to Prince George," he said calmly. "Will I be going home tonight?"

"I don't see why not," Kehler replied. "You'll probably be let off with a couple of speeding tickets. But I want conservation to come and talk to you about this to help us track down where the deer is, help find out where Thomas is, and advise as to the best procedure for your involvement in this."

Kehler stepped out of the backseat of his police vehicle to help Sidhu complete a search of the detained man's truck. It did not take them long to find two crack pipes in the center console and a pipe wrench with blood in its teething diluted in color from melted snow. A four-pack carton of Mudslides was behind the driver's seat. Two had been opened and partially consumed, but the caps had been put back on. Next to them was a four-pack of White Russians. Two of those bottles were missing and the two remaining bottles had been partially consumed in similar fashion as the Mudslides. Kehler and Sidhu spotted a suspicious object on the rear passenger seat: a backpack shaped like a monkey. Both officers immediately wondered why the young man driving the truck would have a monkey backpack. Kehler opened the backpack to look for identification. He found a polka-dotted wallet inside with a medical card bearing the name Loren Donn Toews. The poaching case seemed to be turning into something else.

Kehler needed to keep the suspect in custody until everything could be sorted out. He returned to his police truck and climbed into the driver's seat.

"I'm arresting you for poaching under the Wildlife Act," he told the suspect sitting in the backseat. "Do you understand?"

"Yes," the man answered after a brief hesitation.

Kehler read him the obligatory *Canadian Charter of Rights and Freedoms* warning and advised him of his legal rights, including the right to have legal counsel.

"As of now, everything is on the record," Kehler told him. "I'm just looking for the truth," he emphasized. "I just want to know what's going on here."

"I know what I did was wrong," the man replied with a tone of remorse. "We were poaching, but it's the first time this year."

"Do you poach a lot?" Kehler asked.

"Yeah, I'm a redneck," the man said with a laugh. "That's what we do for fun."

Kehler grinned, and the Good Samaritan in him momentarily took over. He sensed that this might be an opportunity to help someone who had lost his way. He thought he might be able to get the young man back on the right path.

"Look, I'm in my twenties as well," Kehler said, hoping to establish some rapport. "Now's the time to stay on the straight and narrow. What's the pipe wrench – what did you use the pipe wrench for?"

The man took a deep breath and then slowly exhaled.

"We used it to club the deer after we found it to put it out of its misery," he said. "We took turns until it was dead."

Kehler cringed a little despite himself. He imagined the young man clubbing the deer with the wrench, blood spattering in the snow with each thud of another blow. The young man needed more guidance that he originally thought.

"It sounds like you might need some help," Kehler told him. "To beat animals or to watch them suffer – that's what people that turn into serial killers are like. You might need some help," he reiterated.

At that moment, Constable Aaron Kehler had no idea just how close he was to the truth.

"Yeah, I'm trying to change," the man assured him with a smirk. "I'm trying to get new friends."

The two were silent for a moment, for one brief instant no longer an officer of the law and a suspect under arrest, but simply two young men in a perilous world. Presently, the man in the backseat broke the silence.

"Am I going to be able to go back to P.G. and go home?" he asked.

"Yeah, I don't see why not," Kehler replied. "But I do want the conservation officer to talk to you, for direction on how to process this." He gestured at two of the items found in the man's black truck. "Whose crack pipes are those?"

"They're a friend's."

"Well, you won't be getting them back. I'm going to destroy them."

"That's okay," the man said quietly.

Kehler grabbed the two glass pipes and stepped out of the vehicle. He walked to the side of the road, placed them on the ground, and crushed them under his boot with the sound of crackling glass. It was, Kehler would later say, his attempt to cut the young man some slack, to show the man in some small way that he was trying to help him.

| Serial Killer Cody Legebokoff

At around 10:30 p.m., Conservation Officer Cameron Hill was at his home near Highway 27 when the phone rang. After answering the call, he was patched through to Constable Sidhu. Sidhu briefly described the traffic stop Kehler had initiated and advised Hill that they suspected poaching violations.

"Okay, hang tight. I'll be there right away," Hill told him.

Hill arrived at the site of the traffic stop shortly before 11:00 p.m. Sidhu and Kehler briefed him on all of the details of the situation and asked him to take a look at the suspect's vehicle. After a quick inspection of the truck, Hill suggested that he get a statement from the suspect in his police vehicle, which was equipped with a recording device. Kehler agreed and led the arrested man by the arm to Hill's truck.

"What, you don't trust me?" the man giggled. "I'm in the middle of nowhere."

Hill joined the suspect in the truck and informed him that he was investigating the possibility of killing deer out of season.

"Do you mind if I take a recorded statement?" Hill asked.

"No," the man answered flatly.

After again being read his *Charter* rights, the man recounted his story about shooting a deer with his friend, Thomas Russell, and then beating it to death with the pipe wrench to put it out of its misery. Having killed the deer, they put it in the bed of the pickup and took it away to dispose of the carcass. Hill, a seasoned veteran with well over thirty years of law enforcement experience, was not buying it. He suspected that the man was hiding something.

"We're going to find out what really happened because we're going to go down that road," Hill told him, referring to the old logging trail the black truck had first been seen on. "And we're going to talk to your buddy, so if there is something else that happened, you should let us know."

"I told you what happened," the man insisted.

"Yeah, but your story sounds strange," Hill retorted.

"Look, the reason I'm cooperating is because I want to go home," the man said.

Hill ignored the comment. "Why were you only wearing shorts if you knew that you might be hunting?"

"I just threw them on. I was in a hurry."

"So if we do a forensic test, we're going to find that this is deer blood?" Hill asked suspiciously, indicating the red smears on the man's legs and the blood on the Leatherman multi-tool.

"Yes, because that's what it is," the man replied. "I told you what happened."

Hill gave him a doubtful look. "Why were you *really* out here?" he pressed.

"Because my grandpa told me about a hunting area out here."

"But you don't even have a rifle," Hill pointed out.

"No, I was just going down the road to see if I could get in to the area that he was talking about. So I went in, turned around, and came back out."

Hill was still not convinced.

"Look at it from my perspective," he said. "I'm a pretty experienced conservation officer. I do this all of the time. All of these roads are pretty much the same out here. Yet, you drive all the way out here to check out this one particular road?"

"It's not even ten minutes from where I live," the man insisted. "I'm telling you the truth. I'm telling you what happened."

Hill studied the man's eyes for a moment.

"What were you looking for?"

"Anything," the man replied. "Game trails, tracks, any sign of wildlife. I was just scoping it out."

"So I'm not going to find anything unusual when I go out there?"

"No, it's just like I said."

"Have you done this before?" Hill asked.

"Yeah, I've done it before."

"Why?"

"I just like to go shootin.' I don't know what else to tell you. It seems odd, right?"

It did seem odd to Hill, very odd in fact.

"I've never heard of anyone before shooting a deer, killing it with a wrench, putting in a truck, and then going somewhere else to dump it. Why not just leave it there where you killed it?"

"It was in the middle of the road," the man told him calmly. "We didn't just want to leave it there for someone to run into."

A slight scowl crossed Hill's face. The man's story was strange enough, but his demeanor made it even more peculiar.

He was polite and respectful, and more than willing to answer questions, which was not usually the case in Hill's law enforcement experience. Instead of acting nervous like the vast majority of drivers pulled over by the police, the young driver of the black truck seemed almost bored with the situation. He even yawned several times during the recorded interview.

"I know we were breaking the law, but it was just kind of shitty timing," the man said, attempting to lighten things up.

Hill was not in the mood for jokes. He had heard enough.

"Okay, we're done," he said. He took the man back to Kehler's vehicle.

While Hill was finishing up his interview, Constable Sidhu ran a computer check for Loren Dunn Toews. When a missing person's query came back, Sidhu and Kehler looked at each other as the implication of that information sank in. It was clear that someone needed to check out the abandoned logging road that the black truck had first been spotted on by Kehler. Since Hill's four-wheel drive truck was best equipped for off-roading and he was most familiar with the area, he volunteered to check it out. Kehler and Sidhu showed him the road on a map and warned him that, in light of the monkey backpack and missing person report, it was possible that he might find something more than a deer carcass along the road.

Shortly after 11:30 p.m., Hill reached the old logging road. After radioing dispatch, Hill turned his vehicle onto the snow-covered, remote road, following the black pickup truck's tire tracks back into the darkness. New snowflakes were steadily falling as he made his way down the narrow trail. After about 400 meters, the landscape opened up and an old gravel pit came into view. The tire tracks in the snow continued along the west side of the gravel pit, and then abruptly stopped at the southwest end of the pit. Carefully applying his brakes so as not to lose control, Hill stopped his truck just in front of where the tire tracks ended.

About a vehicle's length ahead of him, he saw footprints in the snow. The prints were of differing size and positioned in such a way that it was apparent they had been made by two different people. One person's tracks led from where the driver's side of the truck would have been and the other tracks led from the passenger's side. Both sets of tracks came together at a spot that would have been a few feet in front of where the truck had been parked. Shortly after coming together, the footprints disappeared at an area of snow that had been disturbed.

Hill's heart began to beat faster. He grabbed his flashlight and followed the depression in the snow towards the tree line, expecting to find the carcass of a moose or an elk, but despite his earnestness, it was slow going. The old, accumulated snow was 8 to 10 inches deep with another inch or so freshly fallen, and the narrow, glimmering glow of his flashlight barely illuminated the way.

———

Just before midnight, Doug Leslie was getting ready for bed at his home in Fraser Lake when the phone rang. Leslie, an electric shovel operator for a mining company, had been at an office holiday party earlier that evening, but had come home around 8:00 p.m. When he answered the phone call and heard that it was the RCMP, his heart sank in his chest.

After identifying himself, the police constable on the other end of the line came right to the point of the late-night call.

"Is Loren at home?" he asked.

"No, she's staying with her mother," Leslie replied guardedly. "Why? What's going on?"

"Someone's using her I.D.," the voice on the phone advised. "We pulled over a vehicle on Highway 27 and her I.D. was in it."

"Why . . ." Leslie began to ask, but he was quickly cut off.

"We'll get back to you as soon as we know more," the voice assured him, and then the line went dead with an abrupt click. Doug Leslie hung up the phone, now wide awake and worried beyond words about his teenaged daughter.

The light from Hill's flashlight continued to dim as the batteries began to die. The dull, diminutive yellow of the flashlight's beam barely penetrated the deep blackness of the night that threatened to engulf him. He hurried along as best he could, trudging carefully along the slippery trail in the snow. As he scanned the ground, he noticed some drops of blood and the tell-tale signs of something having been dragged into the trees. The marks from the red-stained snow continued toward the trees and into a dense area of bush until the path became nearly impenetrable. Hill forced his way forward, struggling to keep following the trail. Suddenly, he stopped in this tracks.

"Oh, Christ!" he gasped.

It was just after midnight when he made the gruesome discovery. Among the thickest part of a stand of willow trees, the fading beam of his flashlight dimly revealed the body of a girl lying in the snow, her face battered and mashed, her blonde hair bloodied and matted in discolored clumps of crimson. Being careful to backtrack over his own footprints so as not to contaminate the crime scene, Hill hastened back to his truck. The dismal night suddenly seemed much darker than before.

Immediately after his short discussion with the police, Doug Leslie called his ex-wife, Loren's mother, to see if she knew where Loren might be. A suddenly concerned Donna Leslie recounted how Loren had told her earlier that evening that she was going out for coffee with a friend, but she had not heard from Loren since.

Growing more worried by the minute, Doug called the RCMP dispatch to find out what was going on, but dispatch did not have any new information for him. As the minutes dragged by and turned into hours, he decided that he could not just sit by any longer waiting for the phone to ring. Shortly after 2:00 a.m., Doug Leslie grabbed his car keys and headed toward Highway 27.

Approximately twenty minutes after leaving Kehler and Sidhu to investigate the old logging road, Conservation Officer Hill radioed back to them.

"What happened?" Kehler asked. "Is it what we thought?"

There was a brief pause and crackling of static before Hill's voice came across the radio. Kehler and Sidhu could hear the sorrow in his voice, a deep-seated sadness emanating from the haunting vision of the dead girl, an image now forever imprinted in his memory.

"It's worst-case scenario," he said solemnly.

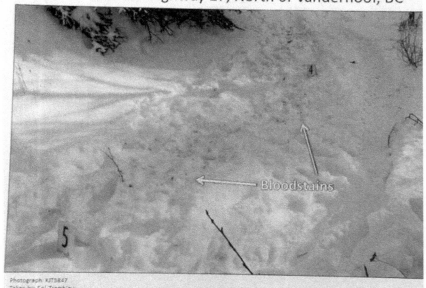

Crime scene Loren Leslie murder

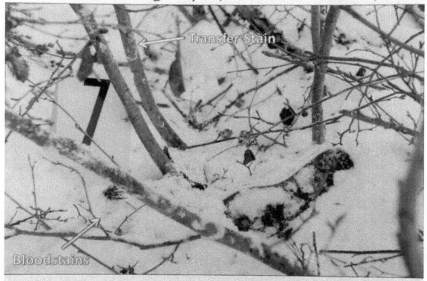

Scene: area off Highway 27, North of Vanderhoof, BC

Transfer Stain

Bloodstains

Photograph: KJT3872
Taken by: Cpl. Tremblay
2010.11.28

| Crime scene Loren Leslie murder

By the time Doug Leslie came upon the scene of the traffic stop, Hill had already rejoined Sidhu and Kehler. Leslie parked behind their trucks and walked over to where they were standing.

"I'm Doug Leslie," he said, "I'm Loren's father. I want to know what's going on and I don't want to hear any bullshit."

Sidhu and Kehler exchanged glances.

"Sir, all we can tell you is that we're investigating a homicide," Sidhu finally replied.

Doug Leslie's knees nearly buckled. He felt like someone had hit him in the gut with a sledgehammer.

Fifteen-year-old Loren Donn Leslie was a Grade 10 student at Nechako Valley Secondary School in Vanderhoof. Brown-eyed with long, blonde, semi-curly hair, and standing about 5 feet 8 inches tall with an average build, Loren was an attractive girl who looked more mature than her true age. She lived with her mother in the nearby village of Fraser Lake. She was sensitive, caring, and compassionate, and she was full of life. But she died in the snow on a remote logging road in the dark of the night.

Although born with a genetic disorder that left her legally blind with fifty-per-cent vision in one eye and no vision in the other, Loren had never let her eye condition limit how she lived. A close friend, Charleine Laing, recalled how most people did not even notice Loren's limited eyesight because she coped with it so well.

"She never let on to it," Laing said. "You would never know meeting her. She did everything everybody else would do and she did it better."

Many of her favorite family activities involved water. She had always enjoyed boating and tubing with her father, and they often made the 90-minute drive to Prince George to spend weekends at a tropical-themed hotel that was a particular family favorite. She was a tireless swimmer and she excelled in karate.

She insisted that people be treated fairly, and she never hesitated to speak up for those who did not speak up for themselves. An entry in her journal evidenced the extent of her compassion.

I hear the loneliness of people sitting in folding chairs at dances because they're not loud enough to be heard, but I hear them, she wrote.

Although diagnosed with depression, Loren often appeared to be happier than most kids her age.

"She seemed to me to be a normal teenager," Doug Leslie recalled. "Most of the time she was quite happy. She seemed like a normal kid."

When she was seven years old, Loren's parents separated, but both parents continued to play an active role in her life, and although she lived with her mom, she had her own room at her father's house as well. Loren's father last saw her at 3:00 p.m. on November 27, the day she was murdered. He recalled that she had looked particularly happy at the time as she walked down the street.

She spent the early part of that evening at home with her mother. Loren passed much of the time on her computer, an activity she always enjoyed, while her mother read in her own room across the hall. At about 8:00 p.m., Loren told her mom that she was going out to have coffee with a girlfriend.

"Okay, be careful, and don't forget to be home by one," Donna Leslie replied, reminding her daughter of her usual curfew. That was the last conversation mother and daughter ever had.

One of Loren's most remarkable attributes was her deep, sincere empathy for others. Loren's grandmother, Kathleen Leslie, described her as a "good little girl" who never hesitated to help others. Her father remembered her in much the same way.

"She was an angel and she still is," her father said, "and she touched a lot of people."

"She cared so much about everybody else," her mother said after hearing the news about her murder. "And I don't know why somebody would do this to her."

| Loren Leslie

At 12:07 a.m. on November 28, Cody Alan Legebokoff was arrested for the murder of Loren Leslie. Though only twenty-years-old, the burly, blonde-haired, blue-eyed Legebokoff had a man's build, standing a sturdy 6 foot 2 and weighing 220 pounds. Immediately after being arrested and handcuffed, Cody turned to RCMP Constable Sidhu. "I didn't tell you the truth," he murmured.

"Don't say anything to me right now," Sidhu warned since Cody had not yet been advised of his legal rights in connection with his arrest for murder.

Despite Sidhu's warning, Cody continued to talk.

"I went there and I found her like that. She was already dead," he declared. "I didn't kill that girl."

Kehler did not respond, but read Cody his *Charter* rights after placing him in the backseat of Sidhu's RCMP truck. Then Sidhu slid into the driver's seat and turned on his truck's audio recording equipment.

"I'm arresting you for the murder of Lauren Donn Toews," Sidhu announced.

"I did not murder anybody," Cody interjected.

"Listen to me, okay," Sidhu continued, "You are being arrested for the murder of Loren Donn Toews. It is my duty to inform you that you have the right to retain counsel in private without delay. You may call any lawyer you want."

"I want to call my dad," Cody replied.

"There is a 24-hour telephone service available which provides you a legal aid duty lawyer who can give you legal advice in private. If you wish to contact a legal aid lawyer, I can provide you with a telephone number. Do you understand?"

"Yeah," Cody replied quietly. "When do I get to call my dad?" His voice began to rise as he continued speaking. "Because I didn't do this. Seen it, yes. I wanted to leave!"

"Do you want to call a lawyer?" Sidhu asked.

"I want to call my dad."

"You have the right to call a lawyer right now. How old are you? Are you an adult?

"I want to call my dad," Cody repeated.

Sidhu checked the age stated on Cody's driver's license. Despite his boyish appearance, in the eyes of the law Cody was a young adult.

"You're an adult so you have the right to call a lawyer right now," Sidhu advised him. "Do you want to call a lawyer?"

"I want to call my dad," Cody insisted.

"Is your dad a lawyer?"

"I want to call my dad," he repeated with growing agitation. "Because I didn't do this."

"You have the right to a lawyer. That's what I'm asking you. Do you want to call a lawyer right now or not?" Sidhu said patiently.

"I want – I don't know why I'm fucking in here!" Cody yelled indignantly.

"I told you, you're under arrest for murder."

"I did not murder anybody."

"Well, I'm investigating a murder. I have reasons to believe . . ."

"But I did not murder anybody!" Cody interrupted angrily. "Found – I found it!" he blurted out in frustration.

"Well, I don't know anything about that right now," Sidhu continued, "so right now . . ."

"Then don't assume that I did murder somebody!" Cody growled.

"Well, I have reasonable grounds to believe . . ."

"Well, I did not!"

Sidhu paused a moment to give Cody time to calm down.

"So do you want to call a lawyer or not?" he eventually asked.

Cody stared out the window into the darkness.

"Yeah," he sighed resignedly.

"Do you have a lawyer?" Sidhu asked.

"My dad would know."

"So you don't know any lawyers?"

"No, I don't know any lawyers."

"Also, you're not obliged to say anything. Anything you say may be given as evidence. Do you understand?

"Yeah. I want to talk to my dad," he reiterated. "Because I did not do this. Drive down the road and find this? It's fucked up."

"Before you tell me anything – you said that you want to speak to a lawyer. We'll get you a lawyer first before you start telling me anything, okay? That's your right. You have a right to speak to a lawyer before you talk to me or tell me anything."

Sidhu started taking some notes.

"What's your dad's phone number?" he asked.

"555-577-5555," Cody replied.

"And what's your dad's name?"

"Bill," Cody said. "My mom might answer too. Her name's Vicky."

"Okay, I'm going to see if I can find you a lawyer."

Cody acknowledged what Sidhu said, but his thoughts were elsewhere. He had always counted on the support of his parents when he needed them. He wanted that reassurance now more than ever.

"Am I allowed to call my parents?" he asked as the reality of his arrest began to fully sink in.

"Not right now," Sidhu replied.

At that moment, miles away, Cody's parents wondered why they had not heard from their son. Never in their wildest imagination would they have guessed what he had done.

| Cody's truck used in murder of Loren Leslie

TWO

Not the First Time

Later that day, a sullen-looking figure sat alone in a small, barren interrogation room, smoking a nearly exhausted cigarette. He had been booked and processed into the Vanderhoof RCMP Detachment by Constable Sidhu, who had also photographed him and taken swab samples from various blood smears on his body. Following the booking process, he had been allowed to call his parents, and shortly afterward he spoke with attorney Bruce Kaun, who had called the police station at his parents' request.

Now Cody Legebokoff stared blankly at the wall, arms folded somberly across his chest. Shortly after 6:15 p.m., the door opened and a lone man stepped into the room.

"How's it going?" the man asked as he closed the door behind him.

"Not too bad," Legebokoff muttered, barely looking up.

The man introduced himself as RCMP officer Greg Yanicki. Part of the RCMP interview team, Yanicki had driven from Vancouver that morning to meet with Legebokoff. Yanicki maintained a friendly demeanor as he made small talk, discussing where the two men were from and trying to establish things they had in common.

Much of the conversation was one-sided, as Legebokoff gave brief, guarded answers to Yanicki's questions. "Yes," "no," and "both" comprised the extent of his typical responses.

Legebokoff remained guarded for the first hour or so, but as the interview continued, he slowly began to open up. He talked about his job at a Ford dealership in Prince George, a city of about 70,000 people, where he had worked his way up from shipping and receiving to a more sought-after position in the parts department. He told Yanicki that he had been employed at the dealership for about a year, and made the move to parts about two months earlier. Legebokoff also provided a glimpse into his relationship with his family when he recounted how he had initially wanted to be a car salesman, but his father convinced him that the parts department would be better for his future since it would provide a more stable paycheck. As his father had pointed out, going into sales might produce a large paycheck one month, but then nothing at all the next. The benefits of working in parts made sense to Legebokoff. He wanted a steady paycheck and a stable future.

As the interview continued, another officer delivered dinner to the room consisting of sandwiches from a nearby sub shop. While the two men ate, they talked about their common interest in fishing, mostly for pike and perch, and joked about funny things that had happened during past fishing trips. Yanicki asked about Legebokoff's educational background.

"My high school had about 150 kids," Legebokoff told him between bites as he wolfed down his sandwich.

"How many in your graduating class?" Yanicki asked.

"Forty-four."

"You a football fan?"

"No – hockey," Legebokoff answered. "I'm a die-hard Calgary Flames fan."

By now, Legebokoff felt comfortable enough to open up about his relationship with his girlfriend, Amy Voell, who he had been dating for several months. Legebokoff explained that they had met at work. She was a receptionist at the same Ford dealership where he worked in parts. Voell was studying English and Psychology at the College of New Caledonia and she hoped to be a teacher after graduating. They planned to move in together at the end of the current semester. Meanwhile, Legebokoff would keep working his way up with the goal of becoming manager of the parts department.

"Sounds like you really got your shit together," Yanicki said, seemingly impressed.

Legebokoff gave a slight smile.

"Am I going to be able to leave here tonight and go home?" he asked.

Yanicki evaded answering the question, but managed to do so without seeming like he was deliberately trying to avoid it.

"The thing is," he said, "you're not a hardened criminal. You're a good kid who comes from a good background and has a life outside of this shit. So the question I have is, 'How did this kid wind up in here?'"

Legebokoff considered what Yanicki had said, and then nodded in silent agreement.

"Look, I'm just trying to understand," Yanicki continued. "How about you tell me your story step-by-step," he suggested.

Slowly, as if weighing each word before giving voice to it, Legebokoff explained how he used to hunt on the abandoned logging road where Loren Leslie's body had been found. On the night of that grisly discovery, Legebokoff had been driving home when he saw some four-wheeler tracks leading off from the highway. He decided to follow the tracks and then came across some blood in the snow. Nearby, he found a cell phone and a girl's bag alongside a heavy pipe wrench and a knife. And the area of snow around the blood had been disturbed.

"It looked as if someone had drug something up into the bush," he told Yanicki.

When he followed the drag marks from the disturbed area of snow, he came across the body of Loren Leslie. She was lying face down on the ground. He rolled her over and immediately saw that she was dead. Her head and face were bashed and bloody.

"I was scared shitless," Legebokoff said, "so I got the hell out of there."

He looked at Yanicki as if trying to read his reaction.

"It was dark and her face was disgusting," he recalled. "I got the hell out of there as fast as I could because I was scared and I have a life. I don't need to be mixed up in something like this."

Legebokoff waited for Yanicki to respond, but the policeman continued peering back at him. He wanted to make sure that Yanicki understood that he had finished telling his version of what had happened.

"And that's the story," Legebokoff added with a sigh.

It was simply a case of bad timing, being in the wrong place at the wrong time, which had led to his arrest, Legebokoff insisted.

Yanicki seemed to be considering Legebokoff's version of events.

"What kind of person do you think would do something like that?" Yanicki asked after several seconds of silence.

"Obviously not a good person," Legebokoff replied.

"What would cause a person to do something like that?" Yanicki again prodded.

"I don't know," Legebokoff said quietly.

Now nearly two-and-a-half hours had elapsed since the interview began. Yanicki ended the session and returned Legebokoff to his holding cell.

A few hours later, Legebokoff was escorted from his cell back into the interrogation room. It was just after midnight. For the next few hours, Yanicki chipped away at Legebokoff's story, trying to get him to provide more specifics, attempting to pin him down to greater detail. At times Sergeant Peter Tewfik, another member of the RCMP interview team, tag-teamed with Yanicki. At one point, Tewfik fished for evidence to link Legebokoff to the murder of 35-year-old Cynthia Maas, a known prostitute and cocaine user, whose body had been found in L.C. Gunn Park on October 9, about seven weeks prior.

The reason we're here talking to you is that I don't think it's the first time. And I think your fear is that we're gonna find out, and I'm telling you, we're going to find out anyway. 'Cause now that we know who you are, we have a starting point. And I'm gonna tell the guys to be diligent and go back over your life, Cody. We're gonna go back over your life. Gonna go back through everything you've done. We're gonna go back through every person, every place that your cell phone goes. We're gonna go back over your records. We're gonna go back over all that stuff.

There are gonna be searches done in your house, of your computer systems, of your phone – we're not done.

Cynthia Maas, that's the body that was found in Prince George here, just a little while ago. And what I'm telling you is that investigation is underway and all they really needed was a starting point for the offender. And there are others and there are DNA profiles that exist and what we're looking for is the offender that's the contributor. And as a result of this offense, we'll have your DNA, and we'll compare it to those and that will tell a story.

Tewfik suspected that Loren Leslie was simply the latest of Legebokoff's victims. He pressed to get a confession.

How many other skeletons are in your closet? Is it one, two, three? Willy was fifty. The Green River killer was way more than that. The Colonel was two, Clifford Olson was somewhere in the neighborhood of fourteen. How many you got in your closet? This isn't the first one. It's just a matter of time until that all comes together. Does that scare you? That we're gonna track back, we're going to find these things? Davey Butorac was three people. Started with one girl, much like you except he was caught on video where he deposited the body, and they found two other profiles in his truck, related to two other victims. How many other profiles are we going to find in your truck? Cynthia – is that just an accident too? Another situation that got out of control?

. . . . .

I don't know, maybe you like that. Maybe you want to be in that league with those people. Maybe that's the reputation you want to have. I don't know. Maybe you like the attention that we're giving you right now.

Now Tewfik tried to play on Legebokoff's pride. His voice dropped deeper in tone to convey the seriousness of what he was saying.

You need to know one thing. Willy Pickton in the press, the pig farmer, was painted as a monster, right? The Colonel killed two women, broke into forty-eight houses, stole a bunch of panties. Kinked up guy, right? He isn't portrayed as a monster. You know the difference between them? The Colonel stood up, said that's what I did, I did these things, I'm gonna take you to this body, it's absolutely me, I did this, this, and this. This is where the evidence is of it. And you know what, Your Honor, I'm guilty. He pled guilty and went to jail. That's the difference between the two. Think about that. Why? Because society wants people to be accountable.

It's no secret, right? People in the community, when

somebody does something wrong, from when you were a kid, everybody wants people to be accountable. That's it. That's what they're looking for. They want you to be accountable.

Be accountable. Help Cynthia's family too.

Tewfik left the room to give Legebokoff time to ponder what he had said. He was hoping his words would appeal to whatever good resided in Legebokoff. Before long, Tewfik returned to finish what he had started.

The reality is, we know you did this one. We're just wondering what else you've got in your closet. And I told you before I don't think this is your first time. That's why we're talking to you and that's why we're here and I want to show you that this is complete because I'm asking you about the others. And I'm telling you that they won't go away because we know who you are now. We found you. And now we can work backwards.

Oh, you can smile, but we can work backwards. We start from you now. We know who you are. You were a mystery to us before, but now we know who you are.

Now we will put that up against all of the other cases that we have. And there are probably other victims that we don't have yet. So if that's what you're smiling about, you're right.

Legebokoff stared back at him with stony eyes.
"I'm not smiling at anything," he said coolly.

THREE

"Not a Monster"

Shortly after 8:00 a.m., Legebokoff was again led into the interrogation room. A bag of breakfast and a cup of coffee from A & W were waiting for him on the interview table. A radio on low volume played country music lightly in the background.

RCMP Sergeant Paul Dadwal introduced himself, and right away Legebokoff could tell that he had a different personality than Yanicki.

"I'll be straight up with you, that's how I roll," Dadwal told him confidently. "I'm not going to fuck with you."

Attempting to put Legebokoff more at ease, Dadwal assured him that he was not a hard core criminal.

"You're a normal person," Dadwal said. "You're not a gangster."

Dadwal had spoken with Legebokoff's girlfriend, Amy, the day before. He described to Legebokoff how he could feel Amy's love for him when she referred to him as a "man," not a "boy." As Dadwal hoped, the mention of Amy's name appeared to break down some of Legebokoff's barriers. He told Dadwal about their plans to marry, have kids, and raise a family together.

"She's the most amazing person I've ever met," Legebokoff said.

They enjoyed an expensive dinner at a Japanese restaurant on their first date, and Legebokoff had recently taken her to Thanksgiving dinner with all seventeen members of his family. He had invited her to share Thanksgiving with his family because, he told Dadwal, "she's the one."

Dadwal sensed a good opportunity to get Legebokoff to talk.

"She loves you and obviously wants to know the truth," Dadwal told him.

"Yeah, but the fact is that I didn't do it," Legebokoff insisted. "I was there, but I did not kill this woman. I was just in the wrong place at the wrong time. I did not kill her because I'm not that type of person. I don't do that."

With more prodding by Dadwal, Legebokoff eventually admitted that did not accidentally stumble upon Loren Leslie's body. In truth, they had met a few weeks before on Nexopia, a social networking website where Legebokoff went by the user name "1CountryBoy." His Nexopia profile included lyrics from country singer Justin Moore's song, "Backwoods," a song celebrating the country lifestyle and the "real good life" he knew in the backwoods.

Legebokoff told Dadwal that on November 27, he had planned on visiting his grandfather and mother in Fort St. James, but arranged to meet Loren at a school in Vanderhoof on his way. After drinking alcohol, they had sex in his truck. Then they decided to go for a ride and talk. He wanted to go off-roading, so they turned down the old logging road. That was when the trouble started.

According to Legebokoff, as they were driving along, Loren suddenly started slapping herself in the face and yelling hysterically how she hated her life. She bitterly shouted that her mom did not care about her and she did not have any friends. Then she screamed for him to stop the truck.

"She started going ape shit," Legebokoff said.

After he stopped the truck, she jumped out and started hitting herself in the face with a wrench that she had grabbed from the floor.

"She just fucking went crazy," Legebokoff told Dadwal. "I don't know what else to say."

She kept hitting herself in the face and head with the wrench until she collapsed onto the ground.

Legebokoff remembered thinking to himself, *what the fuck is going on here?* Shocked at what he had seen, he stumbled out of his truck and wandered over to where Leslie lay in the snow.

"I was so fucking scared," Legebokoff said, "I didn't know what to do."

He grabbed her by the back of her shirt collar and dragged her body about fifteen feet into the bush. He had not explanation for why he moved her there, other than claiming that he had simply acted out of a fear reflex. Now he peered at Dadwal to see his reaction.

"I do have a family and I do have a girlfriend who loves me. And the fact that I would do something like this, it's not right," he said. "I'd never hurt her. I'd never hurt anyone," he insisted.

He also again denied being involved in the death of Cynthia Maas.

"I don't pick up hookers," he maintained. "I don't do that."

Dadwal decided to try a different approach.

"What's your biggest fear right now?" he asked.

Legebokoff looked surprised.

"Obviously going to jail," Legebokoff replied. "It's just a shitty situation. To tell you the truth, I don't know what's going to happen, and it scares me. It does. Because I know I'm not a bad person." Then he added: "Thank you for believing me."

Dadwal's attempts at appearing to be on Legebokoff's side had evidently worked. The more they talked, the more relaxed Legebokoff seemed to be. He told Dadwal that he had been born in Fort St. James in 1990, and had grown up in the small, remote community as well. Hunting and fishing had been his favorite things to do as a boy, and he recounted how he always went fishing with his grandfather during the summers. In school he was not a top-notch student, but not a terrible one either. He graduated from high school with a "C+" grade point average, and his grades would have been higher except that he struggled with math.

"Growing up, I was never mean to anybody," he mentioned as if to lend support to his claim that he had not harmed Loren Leslie. Then he gave Dadwal more insight into his relationship with his parents.

My dad kicked me out of bed early in the morning and said, "Go do something. Go fishing, go dirt-biking, go do something." That's what my life was like. My parents were always good to me. Always. They never once didn't believe me. They were always good to me – always good parents. I'm glad that I had parents who cared.

Every morning my mom had breakfast down on the table waiting. She treated my brother and sister and me like gold, literally. I had a normal childhood really. They weren't strict parents. They just wanted us to succeed. They let us go to parties and go out with friends. As long as I phoned them and let them know where I was at, they were okay with it.

Since Legebokoff was opening up to him more, Dadwal figured it was a good time to press for more of the truth. He told Legebokoff that the detectives working the case had identified some inconsistencies in his story about how Loren Leslie had died. The first inconsistency focused on the fact that when Loren's body was found, her pants and underwear were down around her ankles. Since she had a belt on, her pants would not have just slid down when Legebokoff dragged her body into the bush. Moreover, if he had dragged her when her pants were already down, then the movement would have forced snow into her underwear and pants, but there was no snow there when police located her body. Legebokoff's claim that her pants came down while dragging her did not withstand reasonable scrutiny.

Realizing that his story had been discredited, Legebokoff decided to revise it. Now he told Dadwal that he and Loren had engaged in sex in his truck on the logging road just before she got out of the truck. She was on top, he claimed, and the sex had been fast and a little rough. When they were done, Loren climbed off of him and began to pull up her pants. That was when she started screaming and slapping herself in the face. She hit herself in the face for about thirty seconds before she opened the door and jumped out.

"I'm sitting there watching and going, 'what the fuck's going on,'" Legebokoff told him. "This girl obviously had problems to do what she did."

Dadwal knew that he was making progress in gleaning the truth, but he needed more. He decided to tell Legebokoff another inconsistency that had been found in his story, one centered on the injuries that caused Loren's death. Because of the force of the injuries to her face and the angle at which they had been made, forensic analysis found that it would have been impossible for her injuries to have been self-inflicted. The human arm and hand simply could not bend at an angle that would have enabled Loren to hit herself with a wrench with the force needed to cause the injuries that she had sustained.

Despite the apparent inconsistency of his story, Legebokoff clung to his version of events.

"I know for a fact that I did not kill her," he asserted. "I know that."

After several more attempts failed to get Legebokoff to be more forthcoming about what had really happened, Dadwal asked him if he blamed Loren for the situation that he now found himself in. Legebokoff hesitated for a moment, seemingly surprised by the question. But he did not take too long to respond.

"I blame her for hitting herself in the fucking face," he replied, the tone of his voice clearly conveying an underlying anger.

Quickly collecting himself, he asked Dadwal, "So what will happen? Will they believe my story?"

"Well, you gotta admit that the story is pretty crazy," Dadwal said. "What do you think your parents will say? Do you think they'll believe you?"

"Yeah, I think they will," Legebokoff replied.

After all, they always had before.

Shortly before 7:30 that evening, Amy Voell walked into the interrogation room. Just over five feet tall, the petite, soft-spoken Voell quickly crossed the small room and gave Legebokoff a long embrace.

"What happened?" she asked, still holding him. "Tell me what really happened."

"I want you to know, I did not kill anybody," Legebokoff told her. "I was not raised like that. I didn't kill that girl."

"I know you didn't," she replied.

"I hope you'll find it in your heart to forgive me because I love you, I really do," he whispered to her softly.

Dadwal interrupted the tearful embrace.

"Amy came here to find out what happened," he said. "She deserves to know the truth."

"I know she does," Legebokoff replied, "and I'm going to tell her the truth."

"Why don't you start at the beginning and tell her everything in detail," Dadwal suggested.

Among occasional sobs from Amy, Legebokoff rehashed everything that had led up to his arrest, including how he had come to know Loren Leslie.

"I met her on Nexopia and we eventually exchanged phone numbers," he said. "We met face to face for the first time in Vanderhoof on November 27."

He admitted to Amy that he and Loren had sexual intercourse after they had both consumed alcohol.

"Why?" Amy asked in a state of shock and disbelief.

"You've got to believe me that I'm so sorry," Legebokoff pleaded. "I know this is hard for you to take in."

He looked into her eyes for a few moments as if checking to see whether she believed him.

"I did not kill her." Legebokoff insisted. "I just wish you could find it in your heart to forgive me. I did not kill her. I know that for a fact."

"What happened?" Amy replied, wiping away another tear.

"She just went crazy after the second time we had sex. She started hitting herself in the face. Then she grabbed a wrench from the floor and started hitting herself on the head with it."

"Couldn't you stop her?" Amy asked, her face reflecting a growing sense of fear.

"I was in shock," Legebokoff answered. "I panicked. I didn't know what to do. I was scared."

Amy looked questioningly into his eyes.

"I just hope that you can find it in your heart to forgive me," Legebokoff repeated, "because I do love you."

He told Amy that Loren then jumped out of the truck and started hitting herself again.

"She got out of the truck and that's when the other stuff happened," he said. "I seen the knife and she cut herself with it. I saw the cuts in her throat. She was all bloody. It was a lot to take in. She was gasping and choking on the blood. I panicked. So I got out of there as quick as I could. I just want you to believe me."

As Legebokoff finished his sentence, the door to the interview room opened and Yanicki stepped in, as if on cue to begin a good-cop, bad-cop routine.

"Cody, your story is ridiculous," Yanicki blurted out. "We've had the girl's injuries examined by an expert. You can't beat yourself unconscious. It's literally impossible to hit yourself like that."

He paused for a moment as Legebokoff glanced around the room. Then Yanicki finished his point.

"And a pathologist determined that both sets of injuries, the blunt trauma wounds from the wrench and the cut wounds from the knife, were fatal," he continued. "You couldn't do both to yourself, you could do either one, but you couldn't do *both*."

"I did not hit her," Legebokoff insisted. "I cannot do that to another human being!"

Yanicki let his words continue to sink in. "Tell us the unvarnished, unedited truth," he said at last. "If you panicked and hit her after she'd already injured herself, then just admit it."

"I told you the truth," Legebokoff muttered irritably, his eyes darting from Yanicki to Amy.

"You're being a little naïve," Yanicki asserted. "A person cannot do that to themselves. It's ridiculous."

He glared intently at Legebokoff, and then looked at Dadwal.

"A person cannot beat herself into unconsciousness and kill herself. You can't let him sit here and continue to craft these ridiculous stories," Yanicki told him.

"I'm telling you the truth," Legebokoff murmured.

Now it was Dadwal's turn to play good cop.

"The truth needs to come out now," he said.

Silence enveloped the room until Amy spoke again.

"I love you," she said softly. "And I forgive you for sleeping with that girl. But I'm scared. I love you, but if you're not telling the truth, there's no coming back."

"I told you what happened, you've got to believe me," Legebokoff pleaded.

"Tell the truth," Amy answered, "because if you don't, you're in trouble."

"I don't have the mindset to hit someone with a fucking wrench," Legebokoff said.

Dadwal opened the door and stepped out of the room.

Amy looked at Legebokoff as if trying to read his thoughts.

"You're my Cody and you wouldn't hurt somebody," she said at last. "Would it have been different if I stayed?" she asked, referring to the fact that she had left his apartment after he fell asleep the night of Loren Leslie's murder. It was as if she wanted to share some of the blame for what he had done.

"No," he replied with a sigh.

Amy's mood quickly morphed from guilt to anger.

"I'm mad at you!" she suddenly exclaimed. "I don't understand. It doesn't make any sense, but it's just not you."

Momentarily flustered by Amy's outburst, Legebokoff hesitated before mustering up a response.

"I've never seen something like that before, that's why I was scared," he declared.

"In my heart I know you'd never hurt someone," she replied, still unsure of how she should feel.

"I'm not lying," he assured her. "I love you. You know I love you."

"Cody, your story isn't consistent," Yanicki interjected. "The knife wound by itself would be fatal and the injuries from the wrench would be fatal as well. You couldn't do either one to yourself, but you definitely couldn't do both."

He opened a file folder and read a series of text messages that Legebokoff and Loren Leslie had sent each other, being sure to emphasize Loren's insistence that if they met, sex would not be involved.

"Did you pressure her?" Yanicki asked.

"No, it was mutual," Legebokoff insisted. "It lasted – it doesn't matter how long it lasted. Maybe 10, 15 minutes. Then we left. My intention was to see my mother and grandfather in Fort St. James."

"I was there at your place at 6:30 p.m. and you fell asleep and I left," Amy said, still trying to come to terms with what happened.

"I know," Legebokoff replied. "I had every intention of

going to Fort St. James. That's what I was doing when she texted me . . ."

"Don't lie about what you did," Yanicki interrupted. "What about the drugs?"

Amy's brow furled.

"What drugs?" she asked.

"I did some cocaine before I met her," Legebokoff admitted grudgingly. He turned his eyes away from Amy.

A look of hurt and horror appeared on Amy's face. She frowned and looked down at the floor before fixing Legebokoff with a disdainful stare.

"I'm sorry," she said, her voice rising in outrage, "but you've been lying to me the whole time. I can't trust you anymore."

Yanicki stepped toward the door, stopping beside Legebokoff on his way out of the room. He looked Legebokoff in the eye.

"I'm disappointed that you played me and you played her," he said. "Those injuries simply cannot be self-inflicted."

After Yanicki left the room, it was Dadwal's turn. It was good-cop time again.

"I don't think you're a bad guy, Cody," Dadwal said. "She just did something and you reacted. Something happened that made you panic, made you do something out of character."

He paused a few seconds before continuing. "Why'd you kill her?" he asked. "You're not a pyscho. You're not a monster."

Dadwal opened a file folder and lifted something out of it.

"That, Cody, is not you," he said, holding up a photograph of Loren Leslie's dead body.

Legebokoff studied the photo for a moment and then averted his eyes. He continued to insist that he had not hit Loren with the wrench until after she was already dying.

"I pulled her off the road," he said.

"I'm telling you right now, you hit her with the wrench," Dadwal replied.

"I did not hit her with the wrench," Legebokoff responded, again growing agitated. "You're not a bad guy. You had a good childhood. You're a normal person," Dadwal added as if needing to convince him.

A long silence filled the room as Legebokoff's eyes moved from Dadwal to Amy and then fixed on the floor. Finally, he spoke.

"I hit her," he said faintly. "I hit her with the wrench."

Amy's eyes widened in disbelief.

"How many times?" she gasped.

"Once or twice," he said calmly.

"Just once or twice?" Dadwal asked.

"Twice at the max."

"Walk us through what happened," Dadwal prodded.

"Why do I have to tell it again?" Legebokoff asked indignantly.

"Why don't you want to say it again?" Amy retorted.

"I didn't kill her," Legebokoff said, his voice rising. "She was already dead. But I didn't know what to do when I saw the blood coming out of her. I was scared and I saw the wrench on the ground where she had dropped it. I grabbed it and hit her in the head to put her out of her misery – once or twice at the max. I only hit her after she'd already hurt herself. She was already dead," he stressed.

"We're just trying to wrap things up," Dadwal assured him, hoping to keep the confession moving forward.

"Like I said before, I was planning on going to Fort St. James to see my grandfather and mom," Legebokoff said. "That girl texted me back and forth and I agreed to meet her, and I bought some alcohol for us. Once we got in the truck, we had sex and she said she knew people in Fort St. James. We went up Highway 27 but then went off-roading, and that's when she started going crazy."

He looked tired as he continued.

"I did not see her stab herself. I did hit her a maximum of two times, but I did not kill her."

"Do you know anything about a woman's body recently found in L.C. Gunn Park?" Dadwal asked.

"No," Legebokoff replied sullenly.

Now Yanicki was once again in the room.

"We can't close our eyes to the fact that there are a lot of similarities between what we found off Highway 27 and what we found in the park," Yanicki told him.

"If the DNA comes back with a match, you're going to look like a monster," Dadwal added.

The two investigators stepped out of the room, giving Legebokoff and his girlfriend a few minutes alone.

Legebokoff turned to Amy.

"I need your forgiveness," he said.

"I'm mad at you!" she replied as her eyes fixed him with an icy stare.

"You're the love of my life," he said, his voice growing tender.

"I can't trust you anymore," Amy said sadly. "I believe your story, but I can't stick with you for the rest of my life."

She turned and they shared a long, silent embrace. The look in Legebokoff's eyes made it clear that he never wanted to let go.

Wiping away a final tear, Amy made her way to the door. Without looking back, she opened it and walked out of the room.

FOUR

Dealing With the Pain

News of Legebokoff's arrest brought a brief measure of relief to Loren Leslie's family; however, it did little to diminish the overall sadness they suffered over the tragic waste of two young lives.

The shock that Loren's mother, Donna, experienced when confronted by the news of her daughter's death was compounded when she learned the identity of Loren's killer. Donna had grown up with Legebokoff's grandfather, Roy Goodwin, in Fraser Lake, and she knew that the Goodwin family owned Stuart Lake Lumber, one of the largest sawmills in the area, until they sold it to Dunkley Lumber in what was presumed to be a multi-million dollar deal.

"He comes from a very good family, a very upstanding and decent family," Donna said, referring to Cody Legebokoff. "My first thought was for these other parents. It's horrendous. I just feel so horrible for his family – that's another complete loss, another child, lost. It must be just as horrifying for them."

Loren's father learned that the police had a suspect in custody for his daughter's murder while he was sitting in an interview room at the Vanderhoof police station. Legebokoff was in a cell nearby. When Doug Leslie asked for five minutes alone with Legebokoff, the RCMP officer with him said that it was all he could do not to grant his request. Both men wanted justice for fifteen-year-old Loren.

However, like his wife, Doug Leslie felt sadness over the waste of two promising young lives, and he expressed sympathy for the Legebokoff family.

"It's got to be very hard on them, too," he said, "They're losing a son, just not in the same way."

Cynthia Maas's cousin, Stephanie Apsassin, had a similarly mixed reaction to the news of the arrest.

"It's good – an arrest is very good news," she said, but she was bothered by Legebokoff's young age. "It makes you wonder what he went through, whether he had a difficult childhood."

But Legebokoff's family members echoed his claims of a normal childhood. His grandfather, Roy Goodwin, spoke about the time the two had spent together.

"He had a good upbringing – everything was perfect," Goodwin said. "I hunted with him. I fished with him. We did everything and he was a perfectly normal child. He was no different than you or I when we were younger."

From his parents' perspective, he had been a practically perfect son. His mother had even bragged on Facebook after his high school graduation that he was the "kind of no trouble kid to make a parent proud."

Loren Leslie's funeral took place on Saturday, December 4, in Fraser Lake. By 12:30 p.m., half an hour before the ceremony was scheduled to begin, over 2,000 people packed Stellaquo Hall to capacity. Those without seats stood solemnly in the back of the hall. Loren's favorite song, "Hey Soul Sister" by Train, played through the Hall's speakers while an empty casket was carried in by pallbearers and family members. The open casket was displayed in the Hall's foyer, where many of those paying their respects paused to write a note to Loren on the casket's wooden lid. A memorial in the main room of the hall displayed photographs of Loren along with some of her belongings, including stuffed toys, clothes, and books. Doug Leslie began the service by explaining why Loren's casket was empty.

"She had to be taken to Pennsylvania for further investigation. Holy smokes – it's unbelievable," he said, steadying himself. "But we will be going along as if she's here with us."

During the service that followed, songs were sung, prayers and Bible passages were read, and friends and family members shared their favorite memories of a young girl gone much too soon.

Following an autopsy by Dr. James Stephen at Royal Inland Hospital in Kamloops, Loren's parents allowed her body to be taken to Mercyhurst University in Erie, Pennsylvania, at the request of the RCMP, so that a more detailed analysis of her injuries could be performed by forensic anthropologist Dr. Steven Symes, an expert in examining bone trauma.

About a week after her funeral, Loren's body returned from the additional forensic analysis. Her family held a private cremation service the next day in Vanderhoof. Doug and Donna Leslie each kept one-half of her ashes.

FIVE

More Murders

O n October 18, 2011, following a ten-month investigation that included the assistance of forensic teams in the United States, the RCMP announced that in addition to the murder of Loren Leslie, Cody Legebokoff would be charged with three new counts of first-degree murder in connection with the deaths of 35-year-old Jill Stuchenko, 35-year-old Cynthia Maas, and 23-year-old Natasha Montgomery.

Stuchenko, the mother of four boys and two girls, had apparently been Legebokoff's first victim. She went missing on October 22, 2009. Her body was found four days later, half-buried in a shallow grave in a gravel pit on the fringe of Prince George near Moore's Meadow, an area popular with walkers and joggers located by the intersection of Otway Road and Foothills Boulevard. Forensic analysis of Stuchenko's remains revealed that she had died from a head injury and skull fracture, and much of the rest of her body, including her anus, was covered in bruises.

A man collecting aluminum cans around an area at the lower end of the gravel pit had stumbled across Stuchenko's body at the top of a steep hill. RCMP investigators later learned that the (then) 19-year-old Legebokoff had moved from Lethbridge to 1510 Carney Street in Prince George in August 2009, just two weeks before Stuchenko's murder.

Jill Stuchenko

Maas, the mother of a little girl, was reported missing about a year later on September 23, 2010. Her body was found on October 9 in L.C. Gunn Park in Prince George, an area known to be frequented by prostitutes. Corporal Kent MacNiell discovered Maas's body in a bushy area along a tree line shortly after 2:00 a.m. following a two-hour search. He initially passed by the crime scene despite noticing a very strong rotting smell, which he had attributed to rotting garbage. Like Leslie, Maas's pants had been pulled down to her ankles and she had suffered stab wounds and blunt trauma to the chest, along with fractured ribs, broken cheek and neck bones, and broken fingers. Some of her vertebrate were so severely broken that the damage appeared to have been caused by someone stomping savagely on her neck. At the time of her death, Maas was a daughter, a sister, an aunt, a cousin, a niece, a grandchild, and a mother.

Cynthia Maas

Montgomery had last been seen on August 31 and her body remained missing. The mother of two had a drug habit, which had led to a separation from her long-time boyfriend, a man she had known since she was twelve. However, at the time of her disappearance, Montgomery had made progress in staying sober. She seemed poised and motivated to become a better role model for her children.

Montgomery's father had been in and out of prison during her childhood and had separated from her mother when she was two or three years old. When she was seventeen, she tried crystal meth at school and quickly became hooked, but after six months of rehab, she managed to break her addiction and graduate from high school.

She liked to draw and play music, especially the clarinet and trumpet. She had a warm, welcoming smile and a bubbly personality. Family members described her as a skilled figure skater with a talented singing voice, a "beautiful person, inside and out," someone who made everyone around her feel better.

After the birth of her youngest child in July 2006, Montgomery fell into a cocaine habit, which resulted in her serving time at Prince George Regional Correctional Centre. When her release date drew near, her father sent her a money order so that she could buy a bus ticket to visit him in Penticton. The two had never been close, but he figured it was the least he could do.

On August 19, 2011, Montgomery was released from prison. During their last telephone conversation together on August 26, she told her mother that she was excited to be coming home and that she wanted to be back in time for her daughter's birthday. After not hearing from her daughter for several weeks after that, Montgomery's mom reported her missing on September 23.

| Natasha Montgomery

Our commitment sticks in ACTION!

**Chiefs, and Leadership
Community Search for
NATASHA MONTGOMERY**

Wednesday, September 20, 2017

<u>Schedule of Activities:</u>

8:00 am   Ceremony at Bowren River Rest Stop, 60 km. east
             of Prince George, BC
9:00 am   Press Conference @ Bowren River Rest Stop
             · Louanne Montgomery - mother of Natasha
               Montgomery
             · Chief Wayne Christian – Splat'sin
             · Grand Chief Doug Kelly – First Nations Health
               Council
10:00 am Search plan and schedule for Natasha Montgomery
5:00 pm   Debrief & Feast at Bowren River Rest Stop on
             Hwy 16.

<u>For more information contact:</u>   Chief
Charlene Belleau
<u>250-440-5611</u> (Work) or <u>250-305-8784</u> (Cell) or
charleneb@esketemc.ca
**EVERYONE WELCOME TO JOIN THE
SEARCH**

With the announcement of additional murder charges against Legebokoff, long suppressed feelings of shock and sadness resurfaced in his hometown of Fort St. James, a close-knit community of approximately 1,500 residents.

Mayor Brenda Gouglas noted that the community was once again "reeling" due to the absence of any indications in Legebokoff's past to explain how he came to be a suspected serial killer.

"I picture this as being something so totally out of character for this young man," Gouglas said.

She pointed to Legebokoff's normal upbringing and how highly respected his parents were in the community.

"They're just hard-working, regular citizens in our community who have been here for quite a long time," she noted.

Legebokoff's former teachers were just as bewildered.

"He was a typical kid," said School Superintendent Charlene Seguin. "There was nothing remarkable – I use the word to say that there is nothing that would point us in this direction. Staff members who have worked with the young man in the past are having some difficulty in coming to terms with the news as you would expect."

Harvey Goff, Legebokoff's elementary school principal, remembered him as a "pleasant, hockey-playing fella" who "enjoyed life at school and was liked by most everybody."

Another school official expressed a similar sentiment.

"Cody has a loving family, caring parents and siblings, and

a large extended family in the region," Ray LeMoigne commented. "In school he was well liked by his peers and was very good at sports. He played minor hockey at all levels and belonged to the downhill ski and snowboard teams."

Keith Playfair, a longtime logging company owner in Fort St. James, described the Legebokoff family as pillars of the community.

"They are very good people," he said, adding that the charges against Cody were "hard to swallow."

Commenting on Legebokoff's apparent normalcy, RCMP Inspector Brendan Fitzpatrick aptly described him as "the boy next door."

Though still grieving over the loss of her daughter, Loren Leslie's mother took some small comfort from the additional murder charges against Legebokoff.

"It makes it almost easier because I realize that my daughter's death ended a serial killer's career," she reflected thoughtfully. "Not that it's easy at all, but at least there's some meaning to it."

Loren's father also found meaning in Legebokoff's arrest for additional murders, knowing that at least the families of the other victims might be able to gain some closure.

"I actually feel pretty good about the outcome," Doug Leslie said. "It ties a lot of things together knowing that Loren's case was a catalyst in breaking the other ones."

Friends and coworkers could not believe the news. The Cody they knew had always been such a nice guy, just a normal kid from the Canadian backcountry who enjoyed hockey, snowboarding, and skiing. No one had even the slightest inkling of his dark secret.

Describing the additional murder charges as "quite tragic, quite painful," Brenda Gouglas conveyed the community's general reaction.

"Some of the kids who went to school with Cody are quite taken aback. It's hard for them to believe," Gouglas said. "They had always thought of him as being "perfectly normal.'"

One such school mate was Garrett Anatole. "When my friend told me it was Cody, I couldn't believe it," said Anatole. "He was popular, he got along with everybody, he was fun, joked around, partied and stuff like that."

Another friend made similar comments in reaction to an online story by local television station CPKG:

Cody has always been in the wrong place at the wrong time, and this could have been one of those moments. He is a great buddy of mine, and I wouldn't hesitate for one second to get in a vehicle with him and go cruising. He was my two-stepping partner nights we would go out dancing. I have seen him in bar fights and I have pissed that boy off a few good times, and not once had he ever shown any signs to lose his mind and kill me or anyone else.

Yet another friend noted how, at the time of his arrest, Legebokoff was sharing an apartment with three female friends and he had never showed any signs of violence or aggression.

"He was very sociable and kind-hearted, and he didn't hurt others," the friend pointed out.

Legebokoff's grandfather's disbelief that he had the capacity to commit murder summed up the reaction from his friends and family members.

"The Cody that I know – that I took hunting and fishing – wouldn't do any of that," said Roy Goodwin. "There was absolutely nothing to tell me that he could ever do anything like that. I just don't understand it. Everybody liked him, there wasn't a person that had a bad thing to say about him – nobody."

But Loren Leslie's friend, Charlene Laing, remembered something different about Cody Legebokoff.

"I did not like his eyes," she recalled. "They just looked angry. They don't look soft and innocent. They looked angry."

On the morning of November 29, Legebokoff appeared by telephone conference in Vanderhoof, before being remanded into custody at Prince George Regional Correctional Centre without bail.

The next day, Loki Rulo posted a message to Loren Leslie's family on the internet, expressing his thanks for Loren's influence on his life.

I was friends with your daughter Loren. She helped me through a lot and I never even had the honor of meeting her in person. I live in the states. You and your family have my prayers. And know that Loren won't be forgotten. She was

loved, very much so, by me. I may not have met her in
person, but I was closer to her than any of my friends. I
almost killed myself once and she kept me from doing so. I
owe my life to her. You'll be forever in my prayers as will
the rest of your family.

The additional murder charges against Legebokoff were particularly remarkable because they presupposed that he had started killing as a teenager, unusually early in life for a serial killer. Elliott Leyton, a forensic anthropologist at Memorial University and an expert on serial killers, pointed out the rarity of such a young killer.

"The vast majority of serial killers are between 25 and 55," Leyton said. "Occasionally, there is someone in their 60s, but I have never heard of one in their teens."

As Leyton explained, serial killers rarely begin killing prior to their mid-twenties because the neurological organizational ability needed to maintain a killing career does not develop before then. Moreover, the social and psychological pressures that produce serial killings typically require an escalation period in which they gradually build up during early adulthood.

Members of the public expressed relief at Legebokoff's capture and disgust or outright hatred for his alleged acts. In response to an article about the arrest, one man using the online name "Canadian Warrior3" conveyed a commonly held attitude.

He'll never see the light of day, guys like this cody guy, serial killers that prey on women, or child molesters, they get raped in there. I've been in the pen, I did time for manslaughter, and now I'm a changed man, but if I was still behind the wall, I'd be waiting for his a#$, like every other lifer, RIGHT AT THIS MOMENT.

As the legal process slowly moved forward, family members of Legebokoff's four apparent victims shared memories of their loved ones while trying to make some sense out of what had happened. In response to Legebokoff being formally charged with Cynthia Maas's murder, her family issued a statement that she had a "right to live, to overcome her struggles, to become strong, and to be the mother she wanted to be." On a blog entry entitled, "Love Dad," Loren Leslie's father wrote to his deceased daughter about the impact of the additional murder charges: *Maybe we will have a better idea about what exactly happened to you, and maybe but unlikely, WHY? I am still having a hard time with that.*

To help him make sense out of his daughter's untimely death, Doug Leslie started a foundation in her name. The Loren Donn Leslie Foundation's stated mission is to honor and continue Loren's approach to life: treating others with dignity, compassion, and respect. The Foundation also seeks to raise awareness of the online vulnerability of children around the world so that others will not be victimized by online predators. In the welcome section of the Foundation's webpage, Doug Leslie described the essence of his deceased daughter's personality.

> *Loren, as those of you know who knew her, and those of you who knew of her, was an exceptional young girl. She made no judgment on anyone, she asking nothing of anyone, and she treated everyone with respect no matter who they were. That was Loren's message. Loren was very visually impaired, but never complained about it. In fact, if you didn't know her, you may have never known that she had a visual problem. She coped very well. Loren was a quiet girl, but she listened very loudly, as she stated in her diary. Loren reached out to help anyone that needed help. She asked nothing in return.*

On March 19, 2012, the family of Natasha Montgomery held a smudging ceremony, a traditional First Nation's way of coping with loss and seeking peace. The ceremony took place at the presumed location of Natasha's murder: the apartment that had been rented by Legebokoff at the time of her death. Natasha's family released a statement through the RCMP.

"Today we came here to pray and smudge the apartment where we lost our beloved Natasha. It is hard enough to accept the fact she is gone, let alone not having the ability to lay her to rest. We need her back to help in our family's healing process . . .We wake up every morning wondering if today is the day she is found."

————————————

A few months before Legebokoff's trial was scheduled to begin, "Morgan B," a friend of Loren Leslie's from Kamloops, posted a message to her in the guestbook area of her online obituary being maintained by the *Prince George Citizen* newspaper.

> *Loren, it's so strange to think that you aren't here. Years later it is still hard to believe that something like this could have happened to you. Every now and then I remember silly little things like when our 1st grade substitute teacher told you take off your sunglasses when we came in after recess. She didn't know that you had fancy lenses that changed in sunlight, until the whole class started yelling that she was wrong. I remember the day you and me stayed in at lunch and ripped up our erasers into tiny bits, which we got in trouble for later on. My favorite memory is probably when I went over to your house and the whole time I was there your little sister kept taking my stuffed bear and hiding it. We spent the entire time hunting for it again and again. We never did find it that last time did we? I sure hope you are having fun up there Twinkle Toews.*

SIX

The Crown Presents Its Case

F ollowing jury selection on May 31, Legebokoff's quadruple murder trial began on June 2, 2014, at the Prince George Courthouse in J.D. Wilson Square in downtown Prince George. Supreme Court Justice Glen Parrett, a "formidable character who runs a tight ship and has a delightfully low tolerance for BS," sat as the presiding judge. With twenty-four years of experience as a judge, Parrett had served on the bench for as many years as Legebokoff had been alive.

No longer a baby-faced teenager, 24-year-old Cody Legebokoff appeared in court with a shaved head and goatee, a fiercer look no doubt shaped by his years in prison while awaiting trial.

Crown Counsel Joseph Temple, a distinguished-looking gentleman with a well-trimmed grey beard, and short salt-and-pepper hair, began the Crown's case with a thirty-minute opening statement. He discussed the four murder victims, addressed the circumstances of their disappearances, and at times gave graphic details about the injuries they sustained at the time of their deaths. After laying out the facts about the deaths of Jill Stuchenko, Natasha Montgomery, Cynthia Maas, and Loren Leslie, Temple told the jury members that they would be invited at the end of the case to conclude that all four victims had been murdered by Legebokoff.

Temple also provided details about a series of text messages and Nexopia chats between Legebokoff and Loren Leslie that had led up to their meeting. The texts and chats nearly all began with Legebokoff asking Loren, *What do you like sexually?*, or words to that effect, a question she always ignored or otherwise avoided answering. In one of their last chats, Legebokoff wrote, *How about doggy or anal or are you the type that just likes to get treated like a dirty little whore?* As always, Loren did not answer and instead replied, *Are you actually 20?* Temple told the jury that a few hours before Loren's death, the two exchanged their last series of texts, beginning at 6:04 p.m. on November 27, 2010, when Legebokoff asked Loren what she was doing that night. After some back-and-forth, Loren invited him to come meet her in Vanderhoof and gave him directions to her school.

Don't tell anyone, Legebokoff texted back.

Well, we're just hanging out right? Nothing sexual, Loren asked.

Legebokoff chose not to answer her question.

I'm driving a pickup. Black. I'm wearing shorts, he wrote in reply.

I'm 15, she told him.

I'm 20, he replied.

Want me to get some drinks? he asked.

Chocolate Mudslides, Loren answered.

Temple told the jurors that Loren was seen leaving her home that night just prior to 8:14 p.m., walking and texting on her phone. Later, perhaps growing anxious while waiting for Legebokoff to arrive, Loren texted again.

Where are you? she asked.

I've gotta get alch, he replied.

Hurry. Faster, my ass is getting cold, she joked.

Legebokoff purchased the drinks at 8:20 p.m. Ten minutes later, a witness saw Loren sitting on swings at W.M. McLeod Elementary School in Vanderhoof when a black pickup truck pulled up and parked nearby. As the witness watched, a man in shorts stepped out and started walking towards her.

On June 3, Doug Leslie testified. He identified his daughter's monkey backpack, which had been recovered from Legebokoff's truck the night of her murder, and teared up as he recounted how the police at the crime scene said that they were having difficulty identifying her face due to the extent of blunt trauma and bleeding. He told them that his daughter had the phrase "Grip Fast" tattooed on her wrist in honor of a Leslie family motto derived from a Scottish saying for "hang tight." When officers checked for the tattoo, it confirmed Leslie's worst fear, beginning a nightmare from which he could never awaken.

Donna Leslie also testified, hugging Loren's monkey backpack as she described how much

Loren loved it and wore it constantly. During cross-examination by Legebokoff's lawyer, Loren's parents acknowledged that she had suffered from episodes of depression, but denied that she was bipolar or psychotic, or that she had been suicidal.

During a recess in the proceedings, defense counsel James Heller, physically unremarkable except for a greying, receding hairline, spoke to reporters about his client's demeanor.

"He's taking everything obviously very seriously and he's trying to just really take it all in so he can respond to the situation," Heller said. "He's never been through something like this before obviously, so I guess his demeanor is what you'd expect."

On June 11, Dr. John Stefanelli, an expert in forensic pathology, testified that Loren Leslie had died from "blows to the side of the head and a puncture wound to the neck." He pointed out that the puncture wound was so deep that it had damaged her larynx. Stefanelli also opined that the injuries suffered by Loren could not have been self-inflicted. He paused while looking at one photograph of her injuries and shook his head dejectedly. His voice softened as he explained how he had to shave the side of Loren's head to fully examine her injuries.

"She had quite lovely, long hair," he said sadly.

On June 19, Dr. James Stephen testified about the results of the autopsies that he had performed on the bodies of Jill Stuchenko and Cynthia Maas. Dr. Stephen detailed two lacerations that he found on Stuchenko's head: one at her right ear and one at the back of the head that corresponded to a fracture of her skull. He also found two deep bruises on her forehead and three major contusions to her brain. He testified that "significant force" had been used to inflict the injuries, such force that it would have knocked her unconscious even if it did not kill her outright, and he concluded that her wounds had been caused by at least two different types of weapons. He also noted that extensive bruising on Stuchenko's arms suggested that she had tried to defend herself, most likely by raising her arms in a futile attempt to ward off multiple violent blows to her head.

Turning to his examination of Maas, Dr. Stephen testified that although her body had been badly decomposed with her upper body "basically skeletonized," he determined that the cheekbones and lower jawbone on both sides of her head were fractured, she had suffered a large penetrating wound to her right shoulder blade, and another penetrating wound to one of her vertebrae, her right collar bone was broken, and her voice box had been pierced with a knife or other sharp object. In all, Maas had suffered more than a dozen violent blows from two or three different weapons. Like Stuchenko, bruising on Maas's arms indicated that she had tried to defend herself against the brutal assault of her attacker.

***

As Legebokoff's trial continued, a new page appeared on Facebook entitled "Cody Legebokoff Serial Killer Bring Back the Death Penalty." In advocating for giving Legebokoff the death penalty, the page administrator wondered in writing how many others he had killed in addition to the four women for whose murders he was being tried.

***

Jackie Willard testified on July 22, describing to the jury how she had bought crack cocaine for Legebokoff on four different occasions. In each of those instances, Legebokoff had given her money and then waited in his truck in the parking lot of a McDonald's while she walked to a dealer's house a few streets away to buy the cocaine. Willard became combative during cross examination by Legebokoff's lawyer when he accused her of stealing Legebokoff's money during one of their encounters.

"It's about killing people, not about ripping people off, right?" Willard said. "That's beside the point."

A similar fact witness, Crystal Johnny, testified that she had also purchased crack cocaine for Legebokoff multiple times. On one such occasion, she rode with Legebokoff in his truck to L.C. Gunn Park because he wanted to smoke the cocaine someplace where they would not be seen. After they arrived at the park, Legebokoff's truck stopped running. Since something did not seem right about the situation, Johnny locked the truck's doors after Legebokoff stepped out to look at the truck. Later, when they walked back down the hill towards the main road, she made sure that Legebokoff walked in front of her until they found a pay phone and called a taxi.

On July 24, the Crown called Legebokoff's former girlfriend to testify. As Amy Voell took her seat in the witness chair, the normally stoic Legebokoff lowered his head and briefly appeared to be holding back tears. With prompting by Crown Counsel Temple, Voell told the jury how she had first met Legebokoff in the summer of 2010 at the Ford dealership where they both worked. After they began dating that September, she started going to his apartment three or four times a week, often spending the night there.

She had noticed some stains at various locations in Legebokoff's apartment, but he provided reasonable explanations for all of them. He told her that a bloody handprint on the wall had occurred after he cut his foot one night while drunk, and that blood on a curtain was the result of a nose bleed. He had similar explanations for other stains, including one she saw on a couch cushion.

Voell and Legebokoff had been together for about three months when she spent her final night with him on November 27, 2010, the night of his arrest for the murder of Loren Leslie. According to Voell, she and Legebokoff had both worked at the Ford dealership that day. At 5:00 p.m., her shift ended at work and she went over to Legebokoff's apartment, which was about five minutes from the dealership. They watched television until Legebokoff began to fall asleep on her lap. Around 6:30 p.m., she decided to go home and left Legebokoff dozing on the couch.

When she did not hear from Legebokoff the next day, Voell drove by the apartment building and noticed that his truck was not there. She learned of his arrest when she drove by later and saw police cars in the parking lot.

On July 29, Robert Forsyth, a friend of Natasha Montgomery, testified that he had last seen her on or about August 31, 2010, after dropping her off at a gas station at Queensway and 20th Avenue sometime between 7:00 and 8:00 p.m. She told him that she would be working that section of 20th Avenue and would call him later that night, but he never saw or heard from her again. Forsyth remembered Montgomery fondly.

"She had a great sense of humor," he testified, "and she was smart. She was a lot of fun to be around."

———

On July 30, Sgt. Paul Dadwal took the stand to testify about his interviews with Legebokoff in 2010, and he played the interview recordings for the jury. RCMP Sgt. Beverly Zaporozan, a forensic specialist with expertise in blood spatter analysis who had worked on the infamous Robert Pickton case in 2003, testified the same day. After providing a Power Point presentation on bloodstain pattern analysis, she testified about the specifics of her blood stain analysis of samples taken from Legebokoff's clothes, apartments, and other relevant items. The results of her analysis tied Legebokoff to all four murder victims.

On August 1, the Crown rested its case, having presented 93 witnesses in total.

SEVEN

Legebokoff's Testimony - The X, Y, Z's of Trial

On August 26, as a steady drizzle fell outside the Prince George courthouse, Legebokoff's attorney, James Heller, gave a brief opening statement to the jury.

Ladies and Gentleman of the Jury, you've heard that the Crown has closed its case. At this point, the defense is not compelled to call any witnesses to put on evidence, but it's our election to do that . . . He's going to tell you what he has to say about these charges. And I'm going to advise you right now that there is going to be much that is incriminating and quite shocking in this evidence . . . but he is going to tell you his story. His story is different than the Crown's story. It's incriminating. But he's going to tell you what he wants to tell you about these horrible incidents.

Then Legebokoff rose from his seat and made his way to the witness stand. After swearing to the tell the truth, the

whole truth, and nothing but the truth, the bare-headed Legebokoff settled into the witness chair wearing a suit and tie,
barely resembling the baby-faced boy with curly hair who had
been arrested four years prior. Heller began his questioning by
asking about Legebokoff's family background.

"My childhood was very normal," Legebokoff testified. "I
had normal parents. I got along with both my parents very
well. Ever since I can remember we went fishing every year.
The whole family."

He recalled how they had regularly taken family vacations
together, including twice going to Florida and California.
Asked about his activities growing up, Legebokoff mentioned
a number of sports in which he excelled.

"I was on the snowboard team in high school," he said. "I
played soccer. I played minor hockey for fourteen years. I
played on the Fort St. James Stars."

He described a typical teenager's social life.

"I always had a lot of friends growing up. I had one kind
of serious relationship in high school." He started drinking
alcohol when he was about 13-years old, and later on he began
smoking marijuana. He had also tried magic mushrooms "a
couple times" in high school.

After graduating from Fort St. James Secondary School
and moving away from home, he started meeting girls on the
Canadian social networking website, Nexopia.

"I used it quite a bit," he said.

While living in Lethbridge, he became more sexually
adventurous and had sexual relations with at least six girls.
Some he had met through Nexopia, others he met at area bars,
which he frequented four or five times a week.

After briefly moving back to Fort St. James because he was homesick, he landed a job at a Ford dealership in Prince George, a position he obtained through a family member who knew the General Manager. Having landed the job, he needed a new place to live, and ended up renting an apartment house in Prince George with three girls he knew from home. He had the bedroom downstairs; they had the upstairs bedrooms. Before long they were regularly hosting house parties.

"We had a ton of people show up," he said.

Over 100 people attended some of the parties with both the upstairs and downstairs "packed" with people. It was at one of the biggest house parties that he first met "X."

At this point in Legebokoff's testimony, Justice Parrett looked up with a quizzical expression on his face. He asked for clarification as to whom Legebokoff was referring.

"Explain to the Court what's going on here," Heller told his client, having clearly anticipated that there would be confusion. Legebokoff turned toward the judge.

"There are three people, other people, involved in these charges," Legebokoff began. "And I'm going to name them "X," "Y," and "Z" because, for what I've done, I know that I can get a significant amount of jail time. And that includes going to a federal penitentiary. Guys who give up names to cops are not treated with any respect in prison. I will not go to a federal penitentiary as a rat on three murder charges. That's not in the cards."

"And what do you mean by a 'rat'"? Heller asked.

"A rat is someone who gives up names and testifies in court," Legebokoff replied, and then continued his explanation about "X," "Y," and "Z."

"So I met X at one of our first big house parties through people that I know who also use drugs. That was the first time I started to do cocaine. After that night, he said that if I needed any more, just to stop by his place. And he gave me his address and that's what I did."

During this time period, Legebokoff continued to meet girls online through Nexopia.

"Sometimes they'd stay the night, sometimes they wouldn't," he said.

Heller directed his testimony to the death of Jill Stuchenko.

"Did you have any involvement in the murder of Jill Stuchenko?" he asked.

"Yes," Legebokoff answered calmly. "It was Thanksgiving weekend, 2009. My roommates, Jana and Sadie, left that Friday to go home. Jasmine stayed because she had to work. After that, she went home to Fort St. James as well."

With his roommates all away for the weekend, he went to X's house that Saturday night to buy cocaine. While Legebokoff was there, X asked if he could bring some people over to Legebokoff's apartment later, and Legebokoff agreed. A few hours later, X showed up at the apartment with six other people: three men and three women. They all partied, drinking and doing cocaine. Legebokoff was drinking his favorite lager, Lucky beer. He put on some music, but everyone wanted him to change it to more danceable party music.

"Nobody liked my choice of music because I love country music," he said.

X and Y were on the back couch with one of the girls sitting beside them. Legebokoff sat next to Jill Stuchenko on another couch because he had noticed her when she first arrived with X.

"She wasn't an ugly person, so I figured I'd try my luck and sit next to her," he explained. "I didn't know she was a prostitute at that time."

As cocaine was being passed around to the partygoers on a CD case, he and Stuchenko started talking.

"We started talking sexy towards one another," he told the court.

Soon after that, he and Stuchenko went to his bedroom and had sex. Then they went back into the living room to join everyone else.

"We had sex and that was it," he said impassively.

Later on, he went back into the bedroom, but this time with X and Y. X told him that Stuchenko would have to be killed because she "owed a lot of money to somebody." Without thinking, Legebokoff picked up a pipe wrench beside his bed and handed it to X. X told him to go back to the living room and sit on the couch.

"So that's what I did," Legebokoff said.

A few minutes later, X came out of the bedroom, walked over to Stuchenko, and hit her in the head with the wrench. As Stuchenko fell onto her side on the floor, X hit her a few times more.

"Did you say or do anything?" Heller asked.

"No, I did not."

"What happened next?" Heller inquired.

"I had seen that she was getting blood on the carpet," Legebokoff said nonchalantly. "So I dragged her from the carpet to the laundry room."

He helped X and Y put Stuchenko's body in the back of a pickup truck, and then watched as X and Y drove away.

"That's the last time I seen her," Legebokoff insisted.

After X and Y left, Legebokoff threw Stuchenko's clothes into a dumpster. Then he cleaned up the blood where Stuchenko's body had been.

"How did you feel about what you had just done?" Heller asked, obviously intending to humanize his client by providing him an opportunity to show remorse.

"I knew that what I had done wasn't right," Legebokoff replied, "but there wasn't really much that I could do."

The next day, he drove to Fort St. James and enjoyed Thanksgiving dinner with his family.

"I was a little shaken up," he explained, "but I tried to go on like nothing happened."

A look of vexation appeared on Heller's face, but he quickly shrugged it off and asked his client to explain when he next saw X, Y, or Z.

Legebokoff testified that about a year later, X and Y showed up at his apartment again. This time Cynthia Maas was with them. They all partied and smoked crack like they had done with Stuchenko the year before. Eventually, X and Maas walked over to the side of the room and started talking by themselves. Suddenly, Legebokoff heard a loud cracking sound, followed by a thud as Maas fell to the floor. X reached into his coat and took out a thin object about a foot and a half long, which he used to repeatedly hit Maas in the head as she lay on her stomach on the floor. When he stopped, X looked over at Legebokoff and told him, "This had to be done."

"How did you feel about the fact that this had just

happened in your home?" Heller asked, once again hoping to elicit some demonstration of remorse or empathy from his client.

"Obviously I didn't feel very good, but it was something that had to be done," Legebokoff placidly replied.

After X had finished with Maas, Y said that he knew a place where they could take her body. Legebokoff helped Y carry the body to Legebokoff's pickup truck, and then the two of them drove to L.C. Gunn Park.

"How did you feel then?" Heller asked, still trying to elicit some empathy or emotion.

"I didn't feel very good at all," Legebokoff answered coldly. "When you're smoking a lot of drugs, you don't necessarily care as much about things that you should care about."

Heller knew his client was not making a favorable impression on the jury, but all he could do was continue on.

Legebokoff testified that when they arrived at the location where Y told him to drive, Y opened the truck's passenger door and Maas fell out onto the ground.

"That was when he said that she was still alive."

Upon learning that Maas was alive, Legebokoff reached into the backseat of his truck and grabbed a pickaroon. He handed it to Y.

"Why did you do that?" Heller asked.

"Because he said that she was still alive," Legebokoff responded matter-of-factly.

"What was your point in giving Y a weapon?" Heller continued.

"I figured he was going to use it," Legebokoff replied.

"To do what?"

"To essentially – finish her off."

"Is that something you wanted to do," Heller asked, "you wanted to help finish her off?"

"It's not something I wanted to do, but I didn't know if she was dead at that point or not."

"So?"

"It's just what I did," Legebokoff said calmly. "I passed it to him. And once I did that, I heard him using it. I heard it, I didn't see it because I was on the other side of the truck."

"What did you hear?"

"The sound of the hitting."

"How many times?" Heller asked.

"A few. Three, four times."

Some of the spectators in the courtroom gasped.

When the sound of the pickaroon striking Maas finally stopped, Legebokoff saw Y drag her body off into the bush. He reappeared a few minutes later and they drove away. When Legebokoff returned home, he cleaned up Maas's blood. He never saw or spoke to Y after that.

"Did you have any particular thoughts or feelings about the fact that this X guy had brought you to these circumstances?" Heller asked, still determined to make his client show some compassion.

"At that time, I didn't expect that what I actually did was murder," Legebokoff replied casually. "But eventually I was charged with it and I don't feel very good about it."

Many in the courtroom wondered whether the stone-faced man in the witness chair meant that he did not feel good about the murder or the fact that he had been caught and subsequently charged with it. Irrespective of what Legebokoff really meant, Heller decided that it was time for his client to move on to the murder of Natasha Montgomery.

Telling a familiar narrative, Legebokoff recounted how sometime after Maas's murder, X and Z came over to his apartment with Montgomery and several others to smoke crack. When Montgomery went to the bathroom, X whispered to Legebokoff that she was going to be killed.

"What were you thinking?" Heller asked.

"I was thinking, 'if I don't go along with it, am I dead too?'" Legebokoff replied.

"This is now the third woman killed in your home. Were you thinking anything about that?" Heller said, perhaps hoping his client would realize how incredible his story sounded. The suggestion was apparently lost on Legebokoff, however.

"After all of this happened, I wanted to move out of the apartment and get out of there," Legebokoff replied in the same detached tone he had used to discuss the other murders.

Legebokoff resumed his story by describing how Z had a two-foot long steel bar down his pant leg that was hooked onto the waist of his pants. While Montgomery was out of the room, Z took the steel bar out and handed it to X. When Montgomery left the bathroom and came to the end of the hall, X hit her in the side of the face with the steel bar. Unlike the other victims, Montgomery did not go down right away. Instead, she spun around and ran down the hallway toward the bedroom as X chased after her. X finally tackled her and they both fell to the floor outside the bedroom.

"By that time, me and Z had got up and walked closer and we'd seen Y on top of her," Legebokoff said.

"I'm sorry, *who*?" Heller asked, prompting his client to

think about what he had just said.

"*X*," Legebokoff emphasized in correction. "X was on top of her. Maybe for five minutes or so."

When X dragged her down the hallway to the dining room, Montgomery twitched. Seeing that she was still moving, Z asked Legebokoff for a knife. Without really thinking about it, he grabbed a kitchen knife and handed it to Z.

"I gave him the knife and he used it on her."

"Did you see what he did?" Heller asked.

"Yeah, he cut her throat," Legebokoff answered coolly.

When Z finished using the knife, X asked Legebokoff for a saw. Since he did not have one, he found an axe instead. Legebokoff gave the axe to X, but did not see what he did with it.

"I chose not to look," Legebokoff said.

After a while, X and Z told him that they were going to dispose of the body. They said that he should stay and clean up.

"Did you see how they took her?" Heller asked.

"Yes, she was wrapped up in a sheet. Then they both left."

"Did you see X again after that?"

"Yes, I seen him once, one more time. Quite a bit after. About two weeks later," Legebokoff replied.

Legebokoff explained that when he went to X's house at that time to get crack cocaine, X told him that Montgomery had been killed because "she had ripped someone off and she also owed someone else a substantial amount of money."

"Did you respond to that?" Heller asked.

"I couldn't really respond?"

"What do you mean you couldn't?"

"What was I going to say? I wasn't going to change what

had happened so I chose to leave it at that," Legebokoff stoically replied.

Having covered the first three murders, Heller steered Legebokoff's testimony toward the events leading up to Loren Leslie's death.

Legebokoff began by recounting how he had started dating Amy Voell in late September 2010.

"She was a good girl," Legebokoff testified, but he continued using Nexopia to meet girls online. Loren Leslie was one of them.

"She was one of many girls I was talking to on Nexopia," he explained.

They exchanged phone numbers and started texting each other regularly. At some point, they talked about "hanging out." Loren suggested that he come see her in Vanderhoof, and since he had already planned on going home to Fort St. James to visit his grandfather, he decided to stop by.

He smoked crack cocaine while driving to Vanderhoof, and then stopped at a liquor store to buy some Mudslides and White Russians. After arriving at the school where they had agreed to meet, he parked on a side street and walked over to her. They talked for a little while and then walked back to his truck together. Soon after that, they had sex in the truck.

When he told Loren that he was going to Fort St. James, she said that she knew people there, and he agreed to drop her off at their place. During the drive, she kept complaining that she did not have any real friends and that she was having problems with her mom.

About 20 to 25 minutes into the drive, they came to the old logging road. Legebokoff turned onto it because they wanted to go off-roading. At some point, he parked along the road and they had sex again inside the truck.

"The sex was kinda weird," he said. "It was fast. Just a little strange."

Afterward, things became even stranger.

"She had started hitting herself in the face with her hands at first. And then she managed to get a hold of a pipe wrench and she started hitting herself in the face with it."

He followed her out of the truck and found her on the ground on her stomach. It was then that he saw that she had his knife and had cut her own throat. He panicked and hit her a couple of times with the wrench out of frustration and anger.

"I was pissed off that it came to this," he said, as if explaining why he had kicked over a chair in a temporary fit of anger.

Not knowing what to do, he pulled her body out of the road and into the bush, and then drove away.

"I left in a hurry," he said. "I hit the highway going pretty fast, and when I pulled out to the highway, there was a cop right behind me."

"Why are you telling your story now?" Heller asked.

Legebokoff turned towards the jury before answering. "Because I know what I've done was wrong. And I'm standing before you guys today to tell you guys exactly what I've done wrong. I feel that I shouldn't be allowed to walk out that door as a free man. I know that. But I should not go to prison for what a cop *thinks* I've done."

His direct testimony completed, Legebokoff prepared to face the cross-examination of Crown prosecutor Joseph Temple.

EIGHT

Cross Examination - Poking Holes in the Alphabet Story

Temple began his cross-examination by establishing Legebokoff's pattern and practice of lying to investigators, beginning with the story that he told police after first being pulled over that the blood on his leg and chin, and in his truck, was from a deer that he and a friend had shot. From there, Temple highlighted several inconsistencies in Legebokoff's account of Loren Leslie's murder, including his statement to police that he found her "laying in a big fucking pool of blood." Temple demonstrated that, despite Legebokoff's description of the crime scene, none of the police photos of the crime scene showed any pools of blood, just scattered droplets and smears in the snow.

Continuing the same theme, Temple showed many occasions where Legebokoff had lied to police even when he swore that he was telling "100 percent the truth." He also questioned Legebokoff's account of another aspect of Leslie's death: his claim that Loren's ring finger had been broken when he stepped on her hands while dragging her body off the road, not while she was attempting to defend herself as he hit her with the pipe wrench.

"While you were striking her head with the pipe wrench was she not trying to protect her head with her hands?" Temple inquired.

"No."

"You're saying those crush marks were made on the ring because you stepped on it?"

"Yes," Legebokoff asserted.

"With running shoes?" Temple asked.

"A 250-pound guy stepping on it with rocks underneath the snow, yeah."

"That's your evidence?" Temple asked with obvious sarcasm.

"Yes," Legebokoff answered, his facial expression and tone of voice betraying mounting agitation.

Now Temple underscored another inconsistency in Legebokoff's story.

"You claim that you had sex with Loren Leslie," Temple asked, "but the lab has not found any DNA of yours in her vagina or her anus. What's your explanation for that?"

"Just because they didn't find any semen doesn't mean it wasn't there," Legebokoff insisted. "I know I had sex with her. I'm not a sexual offender."

Temple made a mental note about the last part of Legebokoff's response. He would address it later on in his cross-examination and closing argument.

Next, Temple focused on something Legebokoff had claimed during his interview with RCMP Corporal Paul

Dadwal when he described how Loren had suddenly started attacking herself. Reading from a transcript of the interview, Temple refreshed Legebokoff's recollection about what he had said:

> And the truck had stopped at this point and then she had opened the door. She had got out and like, I was like, like what the fuck, what the fuck's going on. And she didn't, she didn't say anything. She didn't say anything, then she had gotten out and she went over and like, she, she was trying to make a run, kind a like, kind a like, walking, like she was mad and she was hitting herself with this wrench.

Temple glanced at the jury before eyeballing Legebokoff.

"That's a cliché, isn't it?" Temple asked. "You were going to say, 'She was trying to make a run for it'?"

"No," Legebokoff replied unconvincingly, the conviction in his voice much too faint to overcome Temple's suggestion, a suggestion that had resonated clearly in the quiet of the courtroom.

Having demonstrated the questionable nature of Legebokoff's testimony, Temple delved deeper into the details of his role in Loren Leslie's death, the only one of the four murders for which he did not claim any involvement by X, Y, or Z.

"You did beat Loren Leslie to death with a pipe wrench?" Temple asked.

"I hit her in the head with a pipe wrench, yes," Legebokoff admitted.

"She was still moving when you started hitting her?"

"Yes."

"And she wasn't moving when you finished?"

"Yes."

"And you did that because you were very angry with her?"

"Angry – scared," Legebokoff replied.

"There was no Mr. X present when you did that to Loren Leslie?"

"No, there wasn't," Legebokoff acknowledged.

"There was no Mr. Y present when you did that to Loren Leslie?"

"No, there wasn't."

"And there was no Mr. Z present when you did that to Loren Leslie?"

"No, there wasn't."

Although he freely conceded that he was the only other person present when Loren died, Legebokoff became combative at times when asked how her body ended up where it was found. On several occasions, Justice Parrett had to admonish him and instruct him to answer the questions without being argumentative.

"You are arguing," the judge warned him. "If you can address the questions, then do so." Temple handed Legebokoff a trial exhibit consisting of autopsy photos of Loren Leslie. Legebokoff sipped from his glass of water as he flipped through the photos and answered Temple's questions about her injuries.

Having established Legebokoff's lone involvement in Loren's death, Temple targeted the very existence of X, Y, and Z, beginning with the suggestion that, given the brief amount of time that Legebokoff had known them, it would be patently unreasonable to believe that they would feel comfortable murdering a woman – let alone *three* women – right in front of him.

"So in the course of a month and a half you became so well acquainted with a drug dealer, Mr. X, that he elects to make arrangements to murder Jill Stuchenko in your basement apartment in your presence," Temple recited sardonically. "And you expect the jury to believe that you were so trusted by this drug dealer that he was willing to commit murder in your presence after only a month and a half of knowing him?"

"Yeah," Legebokoff said without batting an eye.

"That's your argument?" Temple asked, the sarcasm again evident in his voice.

"Yes," Legebokoff replied, as if baffled why Temple would not believe him.

Seizing on Legebokoff's claim that he could not reveal the true identities of X, Y, and Z because he did not want to be labelled a "rat" in a federal penitentiary, Temple suggested that the real reason for Legebokoff's insistence on the existence of the three phantom men was his desire to avoid being branded a sexual offender.

"In prison, people who commit sexually motivated murders and assaults get even less respect than rats, don't they?" Temple asked.

After pausing but receiving no response from Legebokoff, Temple continued his line of questioning.

"The real reason you won't tell us about Mr. X and Mr. Y and Mr. Z is because they don't exist," he said.

"They do," Legebokoff maintained indignantly.

"And you've made them up so that you can distance your-self from the sexual assault aspects of these deaths . . . "

"No," Legebokoff interrupted.

". . . because you don't want to be in a federal penitentiary as a sexual offender."

Legebokoff glared at him, his cheeks reddening.

"Do you know how many people there are in the federal system that are in for sexual offenses?" he hissed. "A fucking shitload, okay?"

"And you don't want to be one of them?" Temple pressed.

"I'm not one of them," Legebokoff repeated. "I'm not a sexual offender."

Despite further attempts by Temple, Legebokoff continued his refusal to divulge the real names of X, Y, and Z. Even Justice Parrett's direct instruction to answer accompanied by the threat of being held in contempt of court failed to elicit any information about their identities.

"I am not going to be giving any names," Legebokoff steadfastly insisted. "I'm not going to be saying any names."

Temple moved on to challenge Legebokoff's claim that "X" had killed Stuchenko by hitting her in the head with a pipe. He suggested that something else was actually much more probable.

"You hit her on the head!" he told Legebokoff with Perry Mason-like flair. "You stunned her. You punched her just as you described Mr. X did. And then you stabbed her in the neck. Then you watched her as she bled to death on your couch. And then you took her body out in your truck and tried to bury her in the gravel pit."

Legebokoff did not answer, but sat fuming silently in the witness chair.

Temple continued his attack on Legebokoff's credibility by pressing for details about the murder of Natasha Montgomery.

"When you handed Mr. Z the knife, what did he do with it?" Temple asked.

"He cut her throat," Legebokoff replied.

"How did he cut her throat?"

"He cut her throat."

"*How?*" Temple emphasized.

"He used the knife to cut her throat," Legebokoff repeated, once again obviously annoyed at the line of questioning.

"What position was she in when her throat was cut?"

"She was on her back."

"Did he draw the knife from right to left or left to right?"

"I don't know."

"Did he stick the point in and then pull it across, or did he use the edge of the blade and slice down?"

"I don't know," Legebokoff answered with growing agitation. "I don't know."

"How much of her neck did he cut?"

"I don't know."

"Did he cut her throat from ear to ear or did he cut a slice on one side?"

"I don't remember."

"He did this in front of you?"

"Yeah."

"Under your observation?" Temple asked, his voice clearly conveying a tone of disbelief.

"I know he cut her throat," Legebokoff growled back at him. "I didn't take notes or anything on how he did it, which way he did it, how far the cut went, or how far or how deep the cut was. I didn't take those kinds of observations."

"Did it take him one motion or more than one motion?"

"I believe it was one motion," Legebokoff said, regaining his composure.

"What was the result?"

"Blood," he said casually, as if discussing the weather.

After briefly collecting his thoughts, Legebokoff added: "I was under the influence of drugs at the time and wasn't really with it. I just passed him the knife."

Temple eyed the jurors to gauge their response. Satisfied that he had made his point, he turned to specifics about the other murders before finishing his cross examination by underscoring Legebokoff's continuing propensity for telling lies.

"So to sum it up, you lied to Constable Kehler, is that correct?"

"Yeah."

"And you lied to Conservation Officer Hill?"

"Yes."

"And you lied to Constable Sidhu?"

"Yeah."

"And you lied to Corporal Dadwal?"

"Yeah."

"And you lied to Amy?" Temple asked, referring to Legebokoff's former girlfriend.

"Yeah."

"And you're lying to the jury too about Mr. X, Y, and Z," Temple asserted. "They don't exist, do they?"

"Yes, they do," Legebokoff snarled, the resentment in his voice unmistakable.

Temple smiled silently to himself. He knew that he had accomplished exactly what he wanted. He turned respectfully toward the judge.

"Those are all of my questions," he said.

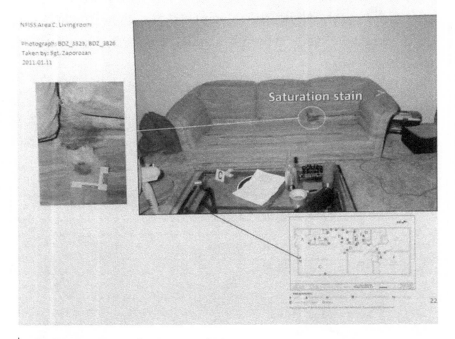

NFISS Area C: Livingroom

Photograph: BDZ_3823, BDZ_3826
Taken by: Sgt. Zaporozan
2011-01-11

Saturation stain

Cody apartment crime scene photo

52 – Master Bedroom

Cody bedroom murder weapon

NINE

The Jury Reaches Its Verdict

O n September 2, Legebokoff's defense counsel presented his closing argument to the jury. In light of the extensive evidence against his client,

James Heller adopted the strategy of acknowledging Legebokoff's guilt, but only with respect to *second* degree murder, not murder in the first degree. Legebokoff's story about the direct involvement of X, Y, and Z allowed Heller to plausibly argue that his client should not be found guilty of first degree murder, which required either planning and intent or murder committed in the course of a sexual assault.

"I'm urging you as his counsel to find him guilty of second degree murder," Heller told the jurors. "I'm conceding across the board that he's guilty of second degree murder."

Heller spent much of the remaining time of his closing seeking to convince the jury that although Legebokoff's story about X, Y, and Z was – admittedly – hard to believe, his willingness to admit *some* degree of guilt in the murders of Stuchenko, Montgomery, Maas, and Leslie should be interpreted as a willingness to take responsibility for his actions. No doubt aware of his client's demonstrable lack of empathy on the stand, Heller also argued that the substance of Legebokoff's testimony should be seen as evidence of remorse for what he had done.

> This is a strange case in a way. You have the defendant testifying and admitting his involvement in the four crimes charged. These are four serious crimes and not just serious crimes, heinous crimes.
>
> . . . . .
>
> Say what you want about him. None of us are in his shoes. As he testified before you at this trial we have his expression and it is such as it is. I would suggest to you that he did, and has, expressed remorse.
>
> It might not be exactly the way that would resonate best with you. It might not be whatever, but in its own way, in his own honest taciturn way, I'd suggest that he did express remorse for these murders. These are four heinous murders and he knows that.

Attempting to use Temple's emphasis on the unbelievable nature of Legebokoff's story about X, Y, and Z in a way to support his client's account of the murders, Heller reminded the jury about Legebokoff's craftiness in lying to the police when he was pulled over and arrested. If Legebokoff could weave such clever, intricate lies *then*, Heller suggested, did it really stand to reason that he could not come up with a better lie *now* – after having had years to think about it – than the tale about the phantom alphabet men, X, Y, and Z?

Heller also submitted another reason why the jury should not find Legebokoff guilty of first degree murder.

"Mr. Legebokoff is not trying to avoid criminal responsibility *at all* based on his drug use and intoxication," Heller said, "but I suggest to you that there should be reasonable doubt as to whether his mental element at the times of these crimes rose to the level of first degree murder." Heller recounted Loren Leslie's psychological condition and mental health history to try to raise a reasonable doubt in the jurors' minds as to whether Loren bludgeoned herself and cut her own throat with a knife, as Legebokoff claimed. Heller wrapped up his closing argument by returning to the overriding theme of his client's credibility.

"How much credibility can he have? That's his real challenge here," Heller acknowledged. "But he could have so easily just exonerated himself." The jury should give him some credit for that, Heller argued.

Next it was Crown Prosecutor Joseph Temple's turn. Having determined to use Legebokoff's questionable credibility as the emphasis of his closing argument, Temple highlighted the inconsistencies and evasiveness of Legebokoff's responses to his cross-examination questions.

"He's not being forthright," Temple told the jury. "He's not giving the answers. He's not telling the truth, the whole truth, and nothing but the truth."

Temple reminded the jury that at the time of Jill

Stuchenko's murder, by Legebokoff's own account, "X" had known him for less than two months. Temple suggested that the jurors should find it hard to believe that "X" would have trusted Legebokoff enough in that short period of time to feel comfortable killing someone in front of him.

"What drug dealer in any resemblance of his right mind would do such a thing?" Temple asked. "That is completely and utterly improbable. It is an incredible, unbelievable story. There's no independent evidence, forensic or otherwise, to support that account."

He pointed out that the significant amount of Stuchenko's blood found on Legebokoff's couch – so much that an "icicle of congealed blood" was found hanging from its bottom – did not reconcile with his story that "X" had struck Stuchenko with a pipe.

"Blood literally poured out of her at the location," Temple stressed. "That means a major blood vessel was severed."

Temple characterized as "just absurd" Legebokoff's contention that Loren Leslie had bludgeoned herself with a pipe wrench and then stabbed herself twice in the throat.

"It's inconceivable that she caused herself massive blunt force trauma and then had the strength and agility left to cut her own throat," he said.

Instead, Temple argued, Legebokoff most likely became angry when she refused to have sex with him, and when she attempted to "make a run for it" from his truck, he chased her down, murdered her in cold blood, and then tried to hide her body in the snow.

"She was beaten with a pipe wrench," Temple told the jury. "Her throat was cut with a Leatherman knife, and she was dragged from the scene of her murder and tucked away in the woods off the road."

Temple urged the jury to reject Legebokoff's claim that Loren's pants came down as he dragged her from the road. The lack of any evidence to that effect made such an event "highly improbable," Temple suggested, just as improbable as Legebokoff's explanation as to what he was doing out on the remote logging road late at night.

"The notion that he went down that road at that time of night because he wanted to go four-by-fouring in the snow is, in my submission, absurd," Temple said.

He suggested to the jury that Natasha Montgomery's body had never been found because Legebokoff dismembered her body in his apartment to aid in its disposal, an idea hatched after he experienced considerable difficulty digging a grave when trying to bury Stuchenko's body the first time he killed. The dismemberment of Montgomery explained why traces of her blood were found throughout Legebokoff's apartment, including his mattress, sheets, and comforter, as well as on an axe recovered from his apartment.

"It turned into a horrible, bloody mess," Temple told the jurors.

After the difficult and messy procedures he experienced getting rid of Stuchenko's and Montgomery's bodies, Legebokoff determined to kill his victims someplace where their remains could be disposed of easier. He took Maas to L.C. Gunn Park to kill her, and having found that method of murder to work nicely, Legebokoff subsequently took Loren Leslie to a secluded outdoor spot as well.

Temple also emphasized the similarities among the four

murders, including the sexual motivations behind them, the types and extent of injuries inflicted on the victims, and how the killer left their bodies. He told the jury that, rather than being "chance or coincidence," they all fell into Legebokoff's "system" for murder, and they all met his criteria for preying on vulnerable victims.

"All four were apparently willing to meet with and associate with unknown males and accompany those males to the male's residence or motor vehicle to consume drugs or alcohol," Temple said.

Tellingly, all three bodies that had been recovered – those of Leslie, Stuchenko, and Maas – showed similar traumatic injuries.

"All suffered massive blunt trauma to the head and upper torso and suffered from multiple blows with significant force," Temple pointed out, adding that all also had significant injuries to their arms or hands, "all likely caused by warding off or blocking blows to the head."

"The Crown submits that it is unlikely to the point of fantasy that all of the similarities that can be observed here have come about by coincidence," Temple emphasized. "Such an explanation does not stand up to a reasonable analysis . . . In my submission you can't look at the results of the attacks and not know that the person who did that was very, very angry."

Such anger, Temple suggested, came about as a result of the victims' refusal to meet their attacker's sexual demands.

"When you look at the amount of damage that was done, it is clear that the person who inflicted that damage was angry."

In the case of Loren Leslie's murder, Temple noted, she had made it clear to Legebokoff that she was not interested in having sex with him. He reminded that jury that in a text message she sent shortly before agreeing to meet him, Leslie wrote, *We're just hanging out, right? Nothing sexual.* Temple suggested that, despite this clear communication of her intentions, Loren's refusal to submit to Legebokoff's sexual appetite enraged him, unleashing the monster who had so destroyed her face that a visual identification of her body could not be made.

Temple also noted how Legebokoff had made a point during his testimony to refer to his girlfriend, Amy Voell, as a "good girl," a conspicuous reference indicating that a distinction existed in his mind between her and the four women he murdered.

Having highlighted the inconsistencies and improbabilities of Legebokoff's testimony and the similarity of injuries to the victims, Temple concluded his closing argument.

Ladies and gentlemen of the jury, in the Crown's submission when you carefully consider all of the evidence in the case you will be satisfied beyond a reasonable doubt that Cody Alan Legebokoff committed and planned and deliberated on the killings of Jill Stuchenko, Natasha Montgomery, Cynthia Maas, and Loren Leslie. And that he committed the murders while sexually assaulting each of these victims. And that he's guilty of four counts of first degree murder.

On September 8, defense attorney Heller informed Justice Parrett that his client wished to plead guilty to four counts of second-degree murder. Temple, in turn, advised that the Crown would not consent to the pleas and would continue to seek convictions for first-degree murder on all four counts. Legebokoff's plea was denied.

After rejecting Legebokoff's attempted plea, Parrett began to instruct the jury about its deliberations, being careful to advise the jury members that while they were "entitled to consider" the pleas as an admission of guilt, they still had to be satisfied beyond a reasonable doubt that all of the elements of first-degree murder were proven by the Crown.

He instructed the jury members that they should find Legebokoff guilty of first-degree murder if they concluded that (1) he committed the murders in a planned and deliberate manner, or (2) the murders were committed during the commission, or attempted commission, of a sexual assault. The judge further advised that in deciding whether Legebokoff had the requisite intent to commit first-degree murder consideration should be given to the alleged level of his intoxication since he testified that he had consumed crack cocaine at the time of each of the four killings.

"As a result of consuming alcohol or drugs a person may not have the required intent," Parrett instructed them. "However, the mere fact that a person's mind is affected by alcohol or drugs so that they lose inhibitions or act in a way in which they would not have done had they been sober is no excuse if the required intent is proven."

After completing his instructions, the judge directed the

court clerk to draw two numbers at random from a box containing the fourteen jurors' numbers. He then dismissed the two jurors whose numbers were drawn, their dismissal the result of legislation allowing extra jurors to be selected in lengthy trials to guard against unforeseen events preventing the required 12-person jury from convening to deliberate.

Just before noon on September 10, the now 12-person jury retired for its deliberations, tasked with determining whether Legebokoff should be deemed guilty of first-degree murder, second-degree murder, or manslaughter, or be found not guilty in each of the four cases.

Shortly before 6:00 p.m. the next day, the eight-man, four-woman jury returned its verdict, finding Legebokoff guilty of first-degree murder on all four counts. As the verdict was read, Legebokoff stood impassively, seemingly oblivious to the foreperson's words.

Justice Parrett announced that he would put off sentencing until September 16 so that he could have time to properly consider fifteen victim impact statements that had been submitted by the families of Legebokoff's four victims. Before adjourning, Parrett instructed Legebokoff to stand.

"Mr. Legebokoff, I am required by law to ask you if there is anything you wish to say prior to sentencing."

"I think I pretty much covered everything..." Legebokoff replied, his voice trailing off into a few more inaudible words.

Family members of his four victims hugged each other,

sharing tears of sadness and relief. Although they were relieved by the verdict, their relief was tempered by a deep weariness and an overriding sense of loss, and they were by no means in a celebratory mood. The loss of their loved ones was still too close in time, the pain still too severe and ever-present. Indeed, Robert Montgomery, Natasha's grandfather, had found the trial much more taxing than he had anticipated.

"I couldn't take it when they were playing the testimony about how he murdered her, about all that he'd done to her, I just broke down," Montgomery said in a wavering voice. "I couldn't take it. I thought I was a big tough guy, but big tough guys fall apart too."

Outside the courthouse, the slow, steady "TOM-TOM-TOM" of First Nations' drummers filled the air along with the soulful, rhythmic chant of the Women's Warrior Song. As the drums and chant quieted, Crown Communications Counsel Neil Mackenzie stepped to a waiting microphone and spoke to the crowd of family members and supporters who had gathered.

> The prosecution recognizes that this has been a long and challenging process for family members to see this case through to this point. And we understand the loss that they've suffered and that the victims of the crimes include the surviving family members and the friends of the women and the young woman who lost their lives. We recognize the loss that has been experienced by people who've lost a daughter, a friend, a sister, or a mother.
>
> . . . . .
>
> Crown counsel also recognize and appreciate the hard

work which was done by police in handling what was a large and complicated investigation and an emotionally demanding investigation.

Next, Inspector Peter Herring, Acting Commander for the North District RCMP division, addressed the crowd.

"We would like to take this time to publicly thank Jill, Natasha, Cynthia, and Loren's families for their support, strength, and patience through this entire case. We respect the emotional impact the investigation and the subsequent trial has had on them . . . All four women were truly loved by their family and friends."

Now it was time for those family members to be heard. LouAnn Montgomery, Natasha's mother, spoke first. She stepped slowly to the microphone. "Oh, God," she gasped tearfully to herself, taking a few moments to regain her composure.

"First of all, I'd like to thank the jury for reaching its verdict. I also want to say that it's not over for me. I still don't have Natasha back," she said, her voice cracking as tears rolled down her cheeks. "And I want to remind the public to please keep an eye out for her remains." Overcome by her emotions, she shuffled away from the microphone, unable to continue.

Doug Leslie felt part of an unseen burden lift away from his shoulders when he heard the guilty verdicts. However, the trial had been a "long haul" for him.

"First of all," he said, "I want to thank the RCMP for their diligence in stopping the perpetrator and finding my daughter and connecting it with the rest of the girls to put this thing to rest. I feel great with the verdicts."

A reporter in the crowd had a question for him.

"Were you offended by this bizarre X, Y, Z story?" the reporter asked.

"How can you be offended with something that's not real?" Leslie replied. "He's obviously, well, who knows. There's no words to describe him. He should never walk the streets again, ever. That's my opinion. And that's about all I have to say right now."

Judy Maas, Cynthia's sister, decided to say a few words as well.

"I just really want to start with saying thanks to the jury. This verdict is bittersweet and at the same time it was extremely scary and we weren't sure how things were going to land. We were very powerless and helpless as we sat here each day. All we wanted in this system is justice. Even though my sister is gone, and we will never get her back, through this we will have a sense of justice."

She steadied herself before continuing.

Our loved ones were more than just a sex trade worker, or a drug addict, or mental health issues. They were truly human beings who lost their way . . . and that's really why we came forward to speak tonight, to say who they were.

. . . . .

They were loved and missed. There's a child without a mother. We have suffered so much in the last four years I cannot even begin to verbalize it adequately from my heart. And we miss them. And how they went was horrendous.

The thought of her sister's death stirred up emotions that were still painfully raw. Steadying herself, she ended with a few words about Justice Parrett.

"I also want to thank the judge," she stressed. "That judge was the best judge I've ever seen."

TEN

"What Resides Within Him" - The
Sentencing of a Serial Killer

On September 16, Legebokoff's sentencing hearing
proceeded in front of a packed courtroom of spectators. Justice Parrett had given due consideration to the victim
impact statements, including Judy Maas's description of the
"excruciating pain" of losing her sister, someone who always
saw the good in others and who had a "never ending trust," as
well as the outraged admonition by Loren Leslie's grandmother that "no human being has the right to take the life of
another." Now, prefacing his findings of facts for sentencing,
Justice Parrett emphasized the emotional burden he faced in
reaching his conclusions.

"Sentencing is among the most difficult tasks the court
must carry out," Parrett said, "and sentencing a young man for
first degree murder is, in some respects, among the most difficult of those."

Having expressed the emotional difficulty of his task,
Parrett delved in the details of the four murders. He started

with Legebokoff's first victim, Jill Stuchenko, noting that "as many Canadians that year were enjoying their Thanksgiving dinner with family and friends, she was dead or dying."

> Ms. Stuchenko had suffered a series of massive blunt force blows to the back and the right side of her head and to her face which caused, in part, scalp lacerations, skull fractures and cerebral contusions. There were multiple bruises from similar blows to her forehead, forearms and upper arms, as well as to both her knees. The amount of blood loss was so extreme that the pathologist had trouble obtaining a sample during the autopsy . . . [T]he extent and nature of her injuries would eventually provide part of the factual basis from which an overall and striking pattern emerged, which, in my view, clearly links the murders of Stuchenko, Maas, and Leslie, and informs and completes the evidence available with respect to Montgomery.

Relying on Sgt. Zaporozan's forensic analysis, Parrett further found that a saturation bloodstain on the couch in Legebokoff's Liard Drive apartment matched Stuchenko's genetic profile, as did bloodstains found in the carpet of the Carney Street apartment where Legebokoff was living at the time of Stuchenko's disappearance.

"After considering the whole of the evidence," Parrett announced, "I am left with no reasonable doubt that Jill Stuchenko was murdered in the accused's basement suite at 1510 Carney Street on the Thanksgiving weekend of 2009 while his roommates were away for the weekend."

The judge next addressed the murder of Natasha Montgomery. Parrett noted that forensic testing found traces of Montgomery's DNA in the shorts Legebokoff had been wearing at the time of his arrest for the murder of Loren Leslie. Moreover, Montgomery's genetic profile matched blood stains found on Legebokoff's bed sheet, comforter, mattress, dining room floor, hallway carpet, bathroom mat, and hooded jacket. And the forensic evidence did not end there. An axe recovered from the entry closet of Legebokoff's apartment revealed fourteen separate matches to Montgomery's DNA.

"After considering the whole of the evidence, I am left with no reasonable doubt that Natasha Lynn Montgomery was murdered in the accused's apartment on Liard Drive, that it was a very violent incident, and that the axe, at least, was used either in the killing or the disposal of her body," Parrett concluded.

Next, he turned to the murder of Cynthia Maas, detailing injuries that were remarkably similar in their brutality to those that had been inflicted on Jill Stuchenko.

"Ms. Maas had suffered a series of massive blunt force trauma blows to her head and face," Parrett said, "resulting in multiple fractures to the facial area as well as fractured ribs, a fractured right clavicle and scapula. In addition she suffered penetrating injuries to the right chest and neck and damage to various vertebrae . . . and a total of sixteen impacts to the skull."

The judge noted that Maas's DNA matched samples taken from a black sweater and white sock found in Legebokoff's truck, a pair of black shoes found in his entranceway closet, and all nine blood samples taken from a pickeroon found in his bedroom.

"After considering the whole of the evidence I am left with no reasonable doubt that Cynthia Maas was murdered and that the pickeroon located and seized from the accused's bedroom was one of the tools used in that murder," he concluded.

Now Parrett addressed the last of Legebokoff's victims, Loren Leslie. Like Maas, Leslie's body had been discovered under trees and partially concealed by heavy brush, with her pants and underwear rolled down around her ankles. The judge noted how "remarkably similar" the "positioning and condition of the body" was in comparison to that of Maas.

Unlike the other victims, the judge pointed out, investigators were able to piece together a "far more complete picture of the circumstances leading up to the death of Leslie" since, unlike the other cases, police had a clear suspect in custody immediately following her murder.

As found by Justice Parrett, those circumstances included a "complete series of text or email communications" between Leslie and Legebokoff that began on November 1, 2010, the first of which included Legebokoff's attempts to persuade Leslie to meet him that evening, the purpose of which appeared to be "purely sexual." Nearly a month later, on November 27, Leslie texted Legebokoff shortly after 6:00 p.m. when his girlfriend, Amy Voell, was still with him. Voell left around 6:30 p.m., and "within a minute" Legebokoff replied to Leslie's text and "began making arrangements to meet Leslie that night."

The "highly revealing" messages that followed included those by Legebokoff urging Leslie "not to tell anyone about him," and her in turn conveying the condition that there would be "nothing sexual" about their meeting. The last text message between them occurred at 8:22 p.m. after Legebokoff purchased Mudslides and White Russians at a liquor store in Vanderhoof. Just after 8:30 p.m., Legebokoff parked his truck beside the chain link fence at W.M. McLeod Elementary School and walked over to the school swings where Leslie was waiting for him. From there, they drove in Legebokoff's truck to the remote logging road off of Highway 27, a trip that took 20 to 25 minutes, putting them there at approximately 9:00 p.m. Within thirty minutes of their arrival, Leslie was dead.

Parrett found that Leslie died from brain injury and blood loss caused by "5 to 8 massive blows to the head" and two stab wounds to the neck. He rejected Legebokoff's claim that Leslie's injuries had been self-inflicted.

"I accept and find that the blunt force trauma suffered by Ms. Leslie was too extensive and severe in and of itself for it to have possibly been self-inflicted. I am also of the view and specifically find that she did not cause the stab wounds to her neck."

The judge recited the numerous items of evidence linking Legebokoff to Leslie's murder, including her blood and DNA on his shirt, shorts, and shoes, her cell phone in his shorts pocket, her blood and DNA on the Leatherman multi-tool found in his shorts pocket, her blood and DNA on the pipe wrench found in the cab of his truck, and her backpack, wallet, and identification found on the passenger seat of his truck.

"After considering the whole of the evidence I am left with no reasonable doubt that Loren Leslie was murdered and that the pipe wrench located in the accused's truck and the Leatherman found in a pocket of his shorts were used by him in the murder."

Justice Parrett concluded that all four murders met the criteria for first degree murder because all four took place while Legebokoff was committing or attempting to commit a sexual assault. With respect to the alternative requirement of being planned and deliberate, he found that the murders of Montgomery, Maas, and Leslie met the criteria, but a reasonable doubt remained as to whether Stuchenko's murder fit into that category since it was the first of the series of murders and nearly a year passed between her murder and the next, that of Montgomery.

Focusing on Legebokoff's testimony that he hit Leslie "a few times" on the head with the pipe wrench because he "was angry" about her behavior and he "wasn't expecting any of this to happen and . . . was pissed off, really, that it came to this," the judge noted a "recurring theme" throughout his evidence, a theme typical of serial killers. "[N]othing is ever his fault," Parrett pointed out. "Things never happen because he does something, they always occur by agreement or mutual consent or for some other reason not directly related to him."

As for the "faceless, nameless individuals" X, Y, and Z, who "pass through crime scenes without leaving a shred of DNA evidence" despite having purportedly murdered three women and disposed of their bodies, the judge found "not a shred of evidence supporting their actual existence." With regard to Legebokoff's stories about the ghostly X, Y, and Z, the judge accepted that Legebokoff was present at the murders of Stuchenko, Montgomery, and Maas, but concluded that "he was the only one there."

After reciting the purpose of sentencing as established under the *Criminal Code of Canada*, Parrett asked Legebokoff to stand and then sentenced him on all four counts of first degree murder to "life without eligibility for parole until you have served twenty-five years of that sentence."

The seasoned judge looked around the crowded courtroom before continuing.

> I wish to emphasize that in each of the three cases in which bodies were recovered . . . the injuries caused in each case were massive and disfiguring, the object of each attack appearing to be aimed at not simply killing the victims, but degrading and destroying them.
>
> For a young man who towered over even the tallest of these victims by something on the order of 8 inches and outweighed even the heaviest by 100 pounds, the use of the weapons he chose was not aimed at any prospect of evening the odds, but at the apparent goal of dominating, degrading, and destroying the targeted victim . . . .

After commenting on the horrific nature of the acts for which Legebokoff was convicted, Justice Parrett seemed to choke on his own words. He paused to take a drink of water, his voice audibly cracking, before resuming.

> These are not the actions of a simple killer, but something infinitely worse. This is a man who by his actions has demonstrated the absolute need to be separated from society

to protect members of that society and, in particular, the most vulnerable members of that society whom he has targeted.

During the two days of his evidence in this trial, Mr. Legebokoff, I believe unintentionally, provided us with a glimpse of what resides within him.

Parrett emphasized that defense counsel's efforts to humanize Legebokoff by repeatedly asking him to explain how he felt after each of the murders "failed miserably." He pointed to Legebokoff's references to the body of Loren Leslie as "it" as providing insight into his "attitude towards his targets and the extent to which he lacks, on any level, empathy or remorse."

It is this "complete void within Mr. Legebokoff," Parrett explained, and the fact that he "lacks any shred of empathy or remorse," which necessitates that he "should never be allowed to walk among us again."

As he came to the conclusion of the sentencing hearing, Justice Parrett ended by recognizing law enforcement's efforts in bringing Legebokoff to trial to face justice, but he also underscored the incredibly fortuitous events that had occurred, without which justice would not have been served.

We should be eternally grateful to a very young and inexperienced police officer whose instincts were sound and on the money. The grief and horrors we heard from the families may well have been simply a precursor to that which would have followed if good luck and fortune had not brought Cst. Kehler to that stretch of Highway 27 on the night of November 27, 2010.

What followed was good sound police work that tried to integrate four separate investigations and bring them to trial.

But make no mistake. It was luck that began these events.

Justice Parrett's closing comments highlighted the frightening truth that it was more than an officer's training that had led to Legebokoff's arrest. Had Constable Kehler come along that remote spot of Highway 27 one minute earlier, his chance encounter with the speeding black truck would not have happened. Had Kehler driven by one minute later, his happenstance arrest of Cody Legebokoff would never have occurred. And a young serial killer's heinous career would have continued well into the future.

After completion of the sentencing hearing, sheriff's deputies began to lead the expressionless Legebokoff away. Suddenly, a man in the courtroom gallery yelled out to him.

"Tell us where Natasha's body is!"

The stone-faced Legebokoff did not look up or respond, but continued walking silently out of the courtroom.

ELEVEN

The Never Ending Aftermath

O utside the grey-domed courthouse, Doug Leslie reflected on Legebokoff's sentence.

"You know, there's a lot of really, really gory movies out there," he told reporters covering the trial. "They don't even come close to what this guy has done. What is he?" Leslie asked, and then as if unable to understand, repeated. "What is he?"

Legebokoff's grandfather, who had spent so many summers with him hunting and fishing, expressed his belief that psychological treatment would be the best way to address his grandson's acts.

"There must be a split personality or something wrong in his head," Roy Goodwin said. "He needs a doctor to help him."

A few days later, on September 19, Teresa Mallam, a veteran newspaper reporter with 30 years of experience covering criminal cases, posted a blog about her time attending the Legebokoff trial. Mallam wrote that she had never before heard "such wicked yet wanting stories" as those detailing how Legebokoff's victims had met their gruesome deaths, stories made worse by the calm manner of their telling by such a "cold and detached storyteller."

Legebokoff's victims are remembered in their own unique ways. The association, Advocating for Women and Children (AWAC), renamed its downtown women's shelter "Cindy's Haven" in honor of Cynthia Maas, who had lived there off and on at various times.

"Cindy had been living here when she went missing, and her murder had a huge impact on all the women of AWAC," said Diane Nakamura, executive director of the organization.

Following Maas's murder, women at the shelter mounted a wooden plaque with flowers outside the room that she used.

Natasha Montgomery's family still longs for her remains to be found so that she can be properly laid to rest, while Jill Stuchenko's family continues to deal with their loss as well.

Loren Leslie's mother had a special deck of playing cards made with pictures of Loren that were taken during happy times in her life. Now Donna Leslie sometimes finds herself playing a game of solitaire just so that she can see her daughter's face.

In February 2015, Legebokoff filed an appeal of his sentence, claiming reversible error for failing to change the trial's venue from Prince George. Doug Leslie believes the appeal to be nothing more than a "last ditch effort," the sign of a desperate man. Prior to the trial, Leslie had wondered how Legebokoff would come across in court. He attended every day of the proceedings, staring Legebokoff down with eyes that screamed for justice. Based on his first-hand observations, Leslie feels confident in describing Legebokoff as an "arrogant, narcissistic sociopath." He acknowledged the reality of Legebokoff's appeal and the possibility of an eventual parole, but he remains convinced that neither is likely to be successful.

"Even people in that situation have a hope to get out," Leslie says. "But he will never get out. In my opinion, he should never get out."

Leslie also sees the good that could come out of the appeal.

> Everything works for a reason, and for us to get awareness out there of what's going on, in reality this is actually a good thing that he's filing this appeal because the public are going to know about that and they're going to become more aware of what he really is. And there are more people like him out there and this is what can, and will, and does happen. So on a positive note, that's the way we've got to look at it.

Expressing his gratitude for Justice Parrett's handling of the trial and sentencing proceedings, Leslie calls him the "best judge in North America." He had been fair, but had also been tough, maintaining control of the proceedings and keeping the participants in line, especially Legebokoff, who had at times turned belligerent when testifying, revealing brief glimpses of the temperamental monster within.

Looking ahead to Legebokoff's pending appeal, Doug Leslie is prepared for the long haul.

"Appeals can go on forever," he said. "But so can I."

Epilogue

L egebokoff was 24-years old when he was convicted of four counts of first degree murder. He was sentenced to serve 25 years in prison for each conviction; however, each 25 year sentence runs concurrently with the other three. Due to Section 745.6 of the *Criminal Code*, Canada's so-called "faint hope clause," Legebokoff will be eligible to apply for parole in 2029, after having served just 15 years in prison. Although the faint hope clause was repealed in 2011 for multiple murders, Legebokoff's crimes occurred in 2009 and 2010, so his "faint hope" endures.

Cody Alan Legebokoff could be walking the streets again as a free man when he is 39-years old.

Acknowledgments

Many thanks to Mark Nielsen at the *Prince George Citizen* for the wealth of information he provided with respect to Cody Legebokoff's trial proceedings. Also, a special thank you to Doug Leslie for sharing memories of his daughter, Loren, and the terrible events that unfolded on November 27, 2010.

Thank you to my editor and proof-readers for your support: Bettye McKee, Lorrie Suzanne Phillippe, Marlene Fabregas, Darlene Horn, Ron Steed, June Julie Dechman, Katherine McCarthy, Robyn MacEachern, and Charlotte Ellis.

About the Author

JT Hunter is a true crime author with over fifteen years of experience as a lawyer, including criminal law and appeals. He also has significant training in criminal investigation techniques. When not working on his books, JT is a college professor and enjoys  teaching fiction and nonfiction in his creative writing classes.

JT is the bestselling author of *The Devil In The Darkness: The True Story of Serial Killer Israel Keyes*, *A Monster of All Time: The True Story of Danny Rolling - The Gainesville Ripper*, and *The Vampire Next Door: The True Story of the Vampire Rapist.*

You can learn more about JT and his other books at www.jthunter.org

A Note From The Author

Thank you for reading *The Country Boy Killer*. Your support means a lot to me!

If you've enjoyed this book, I would be very grateful if you'd take a few minutes to write a brief review on whatever platform you purchased it from.

Reviews are one of the most powerful tools when it comes to book ranking, exposure, and future sales. I have some loyal readers, and honest reviews of my books help bring them to the attention of new readers.

Thank you so much,
JT

Also by J.T. Hunter

Don't miss some of JT Hunter's other True Crime Accounts!

DEVIL IN THE DARKNESS: The True Story of Serial Killer Israel Keyes

He was a hard-working small business owner, an Army veteran, an attentive lover, and a doting father. But he was also something more, something sinister. A master of deception, he was a rapist, arsonist, bank robber, and a new breed of serial killer, one who studied other killers to perfect his craft. In multiple states, he methodically buried kill-kits containing his tools of murder years before returning and putting them to use. Viewing the entire country as his hunting grounds, he often flew to distant locations where he rented cars and randomly selected his victims. Such were the methods and madness of serial killer Israel Keyes. Such were the demands of the "Devil in the Darkness."

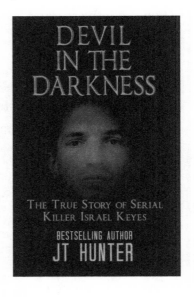

This book is the first detailed account ever published about Israel Keyes. It contains exclusive personal information about this frightening serial killer gleaned from extensive interviews with his former fiancee.

Optioned May 2018 by a Major Production company to be made into a motion picture.

A MONSTER OF ALL TIME: The True Story of Danny Rollins - the Gainesville Ripper

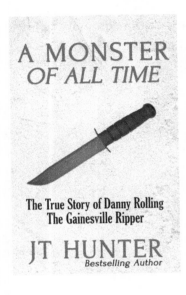

Ambitious, attractive, and full of potential, five young college students prepared for the new semester. They dreamed of beginning careers and starting families. They had a lifetime of experiences in front of them. But death came without warning in the dark of the night. Brutally ending five promising lives, leaving behind three gruesome crime scenes, the Gainesville Ripper terrorized the University of Florida, casting an ominous shadow across a frightened college town.

What evil lurked inside him? What demons drove him to kill? What made him "A Monster of All Time"?

THE VAMPIRE NEXT DOOR: The True Story of the Vampire Rapist

John Crutchley seemed to be living the American Dream. Good-looking and blessed with a genius level IQ, he had a prestigious, white-collar job at a prominent government defense contractor, where he held top secret security clearance and handled projects for NASA and the Pentagon. To all outward appearances, he was a hard-working, successful family man with a lavish new house, a devoted wife, and a healthy young son. But, he concealed a hidden side of his personality, a dark secret tied to a hunger for blood and the overriding need to kill.

As one of the most prolific serial killers in American history, Crutchley committed at least twelve murders, and possibly nearly three dozen. His IQ elipsed that of Ted Bundy, and his body count may have as well. While he stalked the streets hunting his unsuspecting victims, the residents of a quiet Florida town slept soundly, oblivious to the dark creature in their midst, unaware of the vampire next door.

CPSIA information can be obtained
at www.ICGtesting.com
Printed in the USA
LVHW090743180723
752723LV00004B/683

9 780578 711003